Ephesians

Books in the Bible Study Commentary Series

Genesis—Leon J. Wood
Exodus—F. B. Huey, Jr.
Leviticus—Louis Goldberg
Numbers—F. B. Huey, Jr.
Deuteronomy—Louis Goldberg
Joshua—Paul P. Enns
Judges—Paul P. Enns
Ruth—Paul P. Enns
1, 2 Samuel—Howard F. Vos
Job—D. David Garland
Ecclesiastes—Louis Goldberg
Isaiah—D. David Garland
Jeremiah—F. B. Huey, Jr.
Lamentations—Dan G. Kent
Daniel—Leon J. Wood
Hosea—D. David Garland
Amos—D. David Garland
Jonah—John H. Walton
Nahum, Habakkuk, Zephaniah, Haggai
    —J. N. Boo. Heflin
Malachi—Charles D. Isbell
Matthew—Howard F. Vos
Mark—Howard F. Vos
Luke—Virtus E. Gideon
John—Herschel H. Hobbs
Acts—Curtis Vaughan
Romans—Curtis Vaughan and Bruce Corley
1 Corinthians—Curtis Vaughan and
    Thomas D. Lea
Galatians—Curtis Vaughan
Ephesians—Curtis Vaughan
Philippians—Howard F. Vos
Colossians and Philemon—Curtis Vaughan
The Thessalonian Epistles—John F. Walvoord
The Pastoral Epistles—E. M. Blaiklock
Hebrews—Leon Morris
James—Curtis Vaughan
1, 2, 3 John—Curtis Vaughan
Revelation—Alan F. Johnson

BIBLE STUDY COMMENTARY

Ephesians

CURTIS VAUGHAN

ZONDERVAN
PUBLISHING HOUSE
OF THE ZONDERVAN CORPORATION
GRAND RAPIDS, MICHIGAN 49506

Epheisans: Bible Study Commentary

Copyright © 1977 by The Zondervan Corporation
Grand Rapids, Michigan

Library of Congress Cataloging in Publication Data

Vaughan, Curtis.
  Ephesians.

  Bibliography: P.
  1 Bible.   N.T.   Ehpesians—Commentaries.   I. Title.
BS2695.3.V33   227'.5'07   76-44821
ISBN 0-310-33533-7

Printed in the United States of America.

86   87   88 — 10   9   8   7

To my wife MARIAN
and our children
CURT *and* CHRIS
BECKY *and* DAN
and STEVE

Contents

Preface

This volume is a reissue (in revised form) of a work first published by Convention Press of the Southern Baptist Convention. It was used in 1964 as the textbook for a study of Ephesians in the churches of the Southern Baptist Convention.

The volume is designed merely as a *guide* to the study of the Epistle to the Ephesians. It provides a simple outline around which a brief discussion of the text is given. Its aim is to help the reader follow the course of Paul's argument, to point out some of the main emphases of the Epistle, and to stimulate interest for further study.

The *Study Guide* is intended to be used with an open Bible. To realize the most from its study, one must therefore constantly refer to the text of Ephesians.

Ephesians

CHAPTER 1

Introduction

Ephesians is considered by many people to be the greatest of Paul's writings. F. W. Farrar, for instance, called it "the most sublime, the most profound, the most advanced and final utterance of St. Paul's Gospel to the Gentiles" (p. 328). Others think it is the supreme book of the entire New Testament. Indeed, W. O. Carver characterized it as "the greatest piece of writing in all history" (p. 3). In a similar vein, Samuel Taylor Coleridge described it as "the divinest composition of man." With its emphasis on the breaking down of the barriers that divide men and on a reigning God whose purpose for the world must ultimately prevail, surely no book of the New Testament is more relevant to our day.

Across the centuries, Ephesians has nurtured the faith of God's people. Of all the Epistles of Paul, it is said to have been John Calvin's favorite. It must also have been especially treasured by John Knox, for the great Scottish reformer, on his deathbed, frequently had read to him Calvin's sermons from Ephesians. A reading of *The Pilgrim's Progress* suggests that John Bunyan received much of the inspiration for his famous allegory from this Epistle. And a study of a good hymn book shows that the language of Ephesians forms the basis for many of the songs used in our worship.

I. THE CHARACTER OF THE LETTER

To appreciate more fully the message of Ephesians, it is necessary to consider some of the distinguishing features of the letter. Among the more significant are the following:

1. *A Prison Letter.* Ephesians belongs to the prison literature of the Bible, for when it was composed, the author was obviously in some kind of enforced confinement. He calls himself "the prisoner of Jesus Christ" (3:1), "the prisoner of the Lord" (4:1), and "an ambassador in bonds" (6:20). Conservative scholars generally agree that the allusions

are to the period of Paul's first Roman imprisonment. If we assume the correctness of this view, Ephesians must be dated around A.D. 61-63. During the same period of Paul's life, three other letters were written by him: Colossians, Philemon, and Philippians. One cannot be certain of the order in which these were composed, but scholars today generally feel that Colossians and Philemon were written about the same time, that Ephesians probably followed the writing of those letters, and that Philippians was the last of the group to be written.

2. *A Comprehensive Letter.* Ephesians, the most general of all Paul's Epistles, is pervaded by a note of universality. One indication of this is the absence of personal references, local coloring, and closing greetings. But chiefly what we are thinking about is the largeness of its scope. Ephesians has a wider outlook than any other Epistle of the New Testament, with the possible exception of Romans. The sweep of its thought takes in Jew and Gentile, heaven and earth, past and present, and the ages yet to come.

This wide outlook in Ephesians is pointed up by the frequent occurrence of the word *all*, which is found in it more than fifty times. For example, God is said to be working *all* things after the counsel of His will. He is over *all*, through *all*, and in *all*. He created *all* things, sums up *all* things in Christ, and is able to do exceeding abundantly above *all* that we ask or think. Christ sits far above *all* rule and authority and power and dominion and every name that is named. *All* things are put into subjection under His feet, and He fills *all* in *all*.

3. *A Doctrinal Letter.* Ephesians, which contains the last lengthy theological discussion that we have from the pen of Paul, is especially marked by the profundity of its thought. It has much to say about the mystery (the unveiled secret) of redemption and the divine intention for the human race. It treats such majestic themes as the grace of God, the fullness of God, predestination, reconciliation, union with Christ, and the church as the body of Christ. In the words of one scholar, it is "the distilled essence of the Christian religion" and "the most authoritative and most consummate compendium of our holy Christian faith" (Mackay, p. 15). Another says that Ephesians sets forth Paul's "final conception of the meaning and aim of the Christian revelation" (Robinson, p. 14). Carver asserts that "Christian theology has no fundamental teaching that is omitted" from the Epistle (p. 14).

4. *A Practical Letter.* For all its profound doctrine, Ephesians is an intensely practical letter. It comes to grips with moral, spiritual, and domestic problems and gives its answers in clear and unequivocal language. The ethical principles enunciated in the letter are such as to regulate the whole of life, and they have abiding value. These principles are for the most part found in chapters 4-6.

5. *A Devotional Letter.* In Ephesians, as in no other of his Epistles, Paul seems to teach on his knees. This characteristic is particularly true of the first three chapters, where the great doctrinal discussion is cast in the form of a devotional meditation. A. H. Strong, in his *Systematic Theology* (Valley Forge: Judson Press, n.d.), speaks of this portion of the book as having a "psalmodic" quality. Bruce sees in the letter "an inspired mood of meditative adoration and prayer" (p. 15).

6. *A Companion to Colossians.* Ephesians and Colossians are companion Epistles. There are, to be sure, significant differences between them, but the likenesses are even more remarkable. They are alike, for instance, in historical background. Both Epistles were written by Paul while he was a prisoner. Both were intended originally for believers in Asia. Both were entrusted to Tychicus, the messenger who was to bear them to their respective destinations (cf. Eph. 6:21; Col. 4:7). Apparently both letters were written at nearly the same time and were called forth by similar circumstances.

The salutation and general structure of the two letters are similar, and many of the topics treated are common to both. Even the language is strikingly similar. It has been estimated that of the 155 verses of Ephesians over half contain expressions identical with those in Colossians. Ephesians seems to be an expansion by Paul of ideas presented in compact form in Colossians. That Epistle — compressed, abrupt, argumentative — is the sketch of which Ephesians — expansive, meditative, didactic — is the finished picture.

II. The Theme of the Letter

The Ephesian letter is of such nature that it is not easy to decide on one central idea that may be designated as its theme. Some, for instance, understand the key passage to be Ephesians 2:8-10 and take the theme of the book to be the grace of God (cf. Erdman, pp. 14,15). W. O. Carver looks on Ephesians 4:1 as the key verse of the Epistle and affirms its theme to be the Christian calling (pp. 10,21,141). Many interpreters feel that the central theme of Ephesians is unity — particularly the unity of the church as the body of Christ. In this view Ephesians 2:11-22 is the focal passage of the book. But the idea of the unity of the church is simply a part of the larger concept of God's eternal purpose for unifying *all things* in Christ (Eph. 1:10). Accordingly, the letter to the Ephesians may be seen as an *inspired exposition of God's purpose for the whole universe* (cf. Robinson, pp. 18,19; Mackay, pp. ix,x; Bruce, pp. 13-18).

But placed alongside this emphasis on the divine purpose is another strand of thought that centers in the concept of *the people of God.* Throughout the letter, Paul insists that God is working out His great purpose for mankind by calling men to Christ and forming in Christ a new, redeemed society. This redeemed society, which constitutes God's new people, is referred to in various ways in the letter; for example, as God's people (1:2, TCNT), God's heritage (1:11, TCNT), God's building (2:19-22), Christ's body (1:22,23), Christ's bride (5:22-31), the church (1:22; 3:10; 21, et al.), and one new man (2;14,15). The suggestion in all these figures is that God now has a people in the world who belong uniquely to Him. In them His purpose of grace is being worked out, and through them He plans to effect His intention for the whole universe. Thus, the most comprehensive statement of the theme of Ephesians is this: *the eternal purpose of God and the place of Christ and His people in that purpose.* This concept is explained in the first three chapters of Ephesians; the last three chapters show its practical consequences for the Christian life.

FOR FURTHER STUDY

1. Read Ephesians at one sitting, preferably in a translation you have not previously used. Be alert to recurring words and phrases.
2. Read Acts 27 and 28, noting particularly the experiences of Paul in Rome. The writing of Ephesians occurred in the period of time described in the last two verses of Acts
3. Read Colossians at one sitting, noting its likeness to Ephesians.

CHAPTER 2

The Salutation

(Ephesians 1:1,2)

The first two verses of Ephesians make up what the commentaries usually describe as a "salutation." The structure they exhibit was not unusual for letters in Paul's day. The custom was to give the name of the writer first, then to identify the reader (or readers), and finally to express a greeting. Paul followed this pattern in his letters. However, he always gave to the salutation a decidedly Christian flavor and varied and amplified it according to circumstances.

I. THE WRITER (1:1a)

This Epistle, like twelve other New Testament books, begins with the name "Paul." From Acts we learn that Saul was his Jewish name; Paul, it appears, was his Roman name. Very likely he had both names from his birth, but as his missionary work took him more and more into contact with the Roman world, he increasingly used the name that identified him as a part of that world (cf. Acts 13 and 14).

Paul makes two assertions about himself in this opening statement. First, he affirms that he is "an apostle of Christ Jesus." The term *apostle*, a transliteration of the Greek *apostolos*, in its simplest definition means "a person sent," "a messenger." It is found more than eighty times in the New Testament, mostly in the writings of Paul and Luke. In non-Christian literature, the word was sometimes used of a naval squadron sent out on an expedition, or of an ambassador sent out by a government. In the New Testament, the word *apostle* regularly denotes a person engaged by another to carry out a commission. The term is used of Jesus as "the Sent One" of God (Heb. 3:1), of those sent out to preach to Israel (Luke 11:49), and of messengers sent out by the churches (2 Cor. 8:23; Phil. 2:25). But the principal New Testament use of the word is in reference to that select group of men who had a special and direct commission from Christ and who went forth endued with His power and clothed with His authority. In affirming his apostleship, therefore, Paul is asserting his right to address his readers, and in essence is declaring that the teaching he sets forth is invested with divine authority.

Second, Paul declares that his apostleship "is through the will of God."[1] This phrase serves two purposes. In the first place, it emphasizes the divine origin of Paul's commission and thus heightens the thought of his authority. Apostleship was not something he had arrogantly taken to himself; his induction into the office was "not of men" (Gal. 1:1) but was an act of sovereign grace (cf. 1 Cor. 1:1; 2 Cor. 1:1; Col. 1:1; 2 Tim. 1:1). Paul's tone, therefore, is not that of pride but rather of sheer amazement and humble obedience.

In addition, the emphasis on the will of God in reference to Paul's office perhaps shows that he saw his apostleship as a part of God's master-plan (one of the great themes of this letter) for bringing the message of redemption to sinful humanity. (Compare Acts 9:15, where Paul is described as "a chosen vessel" [literally, "a vessel of election"] to bear the Lord's name before the Gentiles and their rulers as·well as before the people of Israel.)

II. The Readers (1:1b)

The persons to whom this letter was first sent are addressed as "the saints which are at Ephesus, and . . . the faithful in Christ Jesus." Three things are to be noticed. First, the readers are said to be "saints." The Greek word, whose root meaning is "separation" or "consecration," means "holy ones." The suggestion is that they are people set apart for the worship and service of God. In the Old Testament the word is used for the people of Israel. The New Testament uses it as a name for Christians. The TCNT therefore renders it by the expression "Christ's people." (Other New Testament terms for God's people are "believers," "disciples," "followers of the way," "brethren," "Christians," etc.)

A popular preacher, speaking some time ago on television, defined a saint as "a Christian who has been awarded a medal of honor for courage and bravery beyond the call of duty"! Such a statement is quite misleading, for in the biblical sense of the word all Christians are saints.

Second, the first readers of this Epistle, according to the text of KJV, NEB, NASB, and others, lived "at Ephesus." These words, however, though found in the great majority of the Greek manuscripts, are not supported by the oldest and best manuscripts of this letter. It appears that Ephesians was originally a circular letter (cf. Galatians, 1 Peter, and Revelation) and intended for all the churches of the Roman province of Asia (of which Ephesus was the capital city). The encyclical character of the letter helps to explain the absence of personal references and the

---

[1]Compare 1 Timothy 1:1, where Paul speaks of being an apostle "according to the commandment of God."

omission of the usual kindly greetings to friends. Apart from the name of our Lord, the name of Paul, and the name of Tychicus (the bearer of the letter), no personal name appears in Ephesians. It is difficult to account for this if the letter was intended solely for the church at Ephesus. (Contrast Ephesians with Romans 16, which is conspicuous for the number of greetings it contains.)

When Paul wrote the letter, he may have left a blank space so that each church, when making a copy of the original, could insert (or understand) its own name. Ephesus was the chief city of the province, the center from which all of Asia had been evangelized (Acts 19:10). The church at Ephesus, being the most important of the area, was likely the first to receive this letter; conceivably, when it had made the round of the churches, the letter was eventually returned to Ephesus for safekeeping. If such was the case, it is understandable that the letter came to be identified with Ephesus. (For other churches in the province of Asia, see Revelation 1–3, in which passage the final biblical reference to Ephesus occurs.)

The city of Ephesus was situated at the mouth of the Cayster River, on the west coast of what is now Turkey. It was approximately 150 miles due east of Athens. Ephesus had from early times been a city of considerable significance, but it was during the days of the Roman Empire that it reached the height of its importance. During this time it came to have the title "Supreme Metropolis of Asia." The city covered a vast area, and its population likely was more than a third of a million. It was the center of the worship of Artemis (Diana), the goddess of fertility. The temple of Artemis (Diana), located about a mile outside of Ephesus and considered one of the Seven Wonders of the ancient world, was the chief glory of the city. Four times larger than the Parthenon in Athens, it is reported to have taken 220 years for its construction to be completed. There was a popular saying to the effect that "the sun sees nothing finer in its course than Diana's temple." The edifice was destroyed by the Goths in A.D. 260.

A third description of the first readers of this letter is found in the words "faithful in Christ Jesus." This designation may mean that they were faithful in the sense of being *loyal* to Christ Jesus (cf. TCNT, TEV). More likely, it means that they were *believers* in Christ (cf. NEB). That is, they were people who had put their trust in Jesus as Messiah and Savior. The expression "in Christ Jesus" suggests not only that He was the object of their faith but also that they enjoyed a living union with Him. Indeed, it was by virtue of this union that they were "saints" and "believers."

Those interpreters are probably correct who understand "the saints . . . and . . . the faithful" as a unity. That is to say, the same persons are designated by the two terms. The Greek might be rendered "the saints and believers who are in Ephesus in Christ Jesus" (cf. Hendriksen, p. 70).

III. THE GREETING (1:2)

Paul's greeting is in the form of a prayer. In it he wishes for all his readers "grace" and "peace" from God. The usual Greek salutation was "rejoice!" (*chairein*). Paul replaces this by a similar-sounding word (*charis*, "grace") and adds to it the usual Jewish greeting: "peace." Grace is God's free, loving favor lavished on the undeserving. "Peace," which is a consequence of experiencing God's favor, signified not simply the absence of strife but the presence of positive blessings. The word denotes wholeness, soundness, or prosperity, especially in spiritual things. It conveys essentially the idea of 3 John 2: "I pray that in all things thou mayest prosper and be in health, even as thy soul prospereth" (ASV).

Both grace and peace come from "God our Father and the Lord Jesus Christ" (RSV). Salmond speaks of this as "a collocation impossible except on the supposition that the writer held Christ to be of the same rank with God or in a unique relation to Him" (p. 244). The distinction suggested is not a distinction in nature but one in respect of relation to believers. The one is related to them as Father, the other as Lord.

FOR FURTHER STUDY

1. Locate Ephesus on a map of the biblical world. Good maps may be found in *The Zondervan Pictorial Bible Atlas* (ed. E. M. Blaiklock) and *The Westminster Bible Atlas* (ed. G. E. Wright and F. V. Filson). An excellent map, entitled "Lands of the Bible Today," is available from the National Geographic Society.

2. Read Acts 19 and learn all you can about how the church at Ephesus was begun; read Acts 20:17-38 and learn of Paul's concern for the church.

3. Compare the first two verses of Ephesians with the opening verses of other of Paul's Epistles.

4. Using a Bible dictionary, read articles on "Ephesians," "Paul," "apostle," and the Roman imprisonment of Paul. (A useful one-volume dictionary is *The Zondervan Pictorial Bible Dictionary*.)

CHAPTER 3

The Blessings of God's
New People: A Doxology

(Ephesians 1:3-14)

Most of Paul's Epistles begin with an expression of thanks to God for certain spiritual qualities produced by divine grace and power in the readers' lives (cf. Rom. 1:8ff.; 1 Cor. 1:4ff.; Phil. 1:3ff.; Col. 1:3ff., et al.). Ephesians, however, is different. Here, instead of the customary thanksgiving, there is what more appropriately may be called a doxology — a majestic hymn of praise to God. (The thanksgiving, to be sure, is eventually brought in [cf. 1:15], but, as Robinson says, "not until the great doxology has run its full course" [p. 23].)

This outburst of adoring praise requires and rewards the closest study. Two matters should be considered before we attempt to interpret it. The first is its *structure*. In the Greek text verses 3-14 constitute one magnificent sentence intricately and skillfully put together. The kjv, to help the reader keep the connection of thought, places a period at the end of verses 6, 12, and 14. Following this punctuation, one may think of Paul's inspired hymn as falling into three stanzas. The first (vss. 3-6) relates to the past and centers largely in the gracious purpose of the Father. The second (vss. 7-12) has to do with the present and revolves mainly around the redemptive work of Christ. The third (vss. 13,14) points to the future consummation of redemption and magnifies the ministry of the Holy Spirit. Each stanza closes with a refrain: "to the praise of the glory of his grace" (vs. 6), "to the praise of his glory" (vs. 12), "unto the praise of his glory" (vs. 14).

The second matter to consider is the *theme*. The entire passage, throbbing with a sense of the majesty and goodness of God, may be seen as an ascription of praise to Him for His gracious benefits to His people. This note, which resounds throughout the paragraph, is first struck in verse 3: "Blessed be . . . God, . . . who hath blessed us with all spiritual blessings." Notice the joyous and emphatic reiteration: "blessed," "hath blessed," "blessings." It is reminiscent of Psalm 103: "Bless the LORD, O my soul; and all that is within me, bless his holy name. Bless the Lord, O my soul, and forget not all his benefits" (vss. 1,2).

"Blessed" translates an adjective used in the New Testament exclusively of God. (Cf., e.g., Mark 14:61; Luke 1:68; Rom. 9:5; 2 Cor. 1:3; 1 Peter 1:3.) The inference is that He alone has an unchanging claim on our homage. In "blessing" God we do not, of course, add anything to Him or bestow any benefit on Him. We simply acknowledge His mercy and offer praise and thanks to Him for His goodness to us. The Greek word means "to be praised," "worthy of praise." "Praise be to the God and Father of our Lord Jesus Christ" (NIV).

"Hath blessed" translates a verb the tense of which sums up all the blessings of God and treats them as a single whole. The primary reference appears to be to those blessings that come to the believer in his experience of conversion, but the concept is broad enough to include every act of divine blessing.

Our blessing (praising) of God, it is implied, is in response to the blessings (benefits) we have received from Him. Those blessings are *described* in verses 3-6, and some of the principal ones are *enumerated* in verses 7-14.

I. A Description of the Divine Blessings (1:3-6).

One of the richest and most overwhelming passages in the Bible is this discussion of the blessings that are ours in Christ Jesus. Calvin speaks of the "lofty terms" employed and explains that they are intended to rouse believers' hearts to gratitude, "to set them all on flame, to fill them even to overflowing with this disposition."

1. *Their Character* (vs. 3). God has blessed us "with all spiritual blessings" (vs. 3). Some think the word "spiritual" is used to emphasize that our blessings are derived from the Spirit and communicated to us by Him. These blessings do, of course, come from the Spirit, and are realized in us only through His work, but it is doubtful that the apostle had this in mind in using the word "spiritual." Paul's term emphasizes, not the source of our blessings, but their nature. That is, they are spiritual rather than natural or material. Paul, a childless, landless, homeless man, knew little of material blessings, but in regard to things spiritual he knew himself to have boundless wealth. The contemplation of these blessings opened in his heart the floodgates of grateful praise.

"All spiritual blessings" is taken by some to mean that there is no spiritual blessing that we have that does not come from God. This is of course true, but perhaps it is better to understand the word in the sense of "every kind of." Whatever our spiritual lives require, God amply and abundantly provides. He has given us "every possible benefit in Christ!" (vs. 3, Phillips).

2. *The Sphere in Which They Are Experienced* (vs. 3). Two expres-

sions define the sphere in which God's people are blessed. One is the phrase "in heavenly places" (vs. 3; literally, "in the heavenlies"). This unusual expression occurs five times in Ephesians (1:3,20; 2:6; 3:10; 6:12, ASV) but nowhere else in the New Testament. To determine its meaning, one should study carefully each passage where it is used. In 1:20 it is the sphere to which the risen Christ has been exalted and enthroned; in 2:6 it is the region to which believers have been lifted in fellowship with Christ; in 3:10 it is where principalities and powers learn of the wisdom of God as exhibited through His people; in 6:12 it is the spiritual battleground where believers confront the forces of wickedness. It appears, then, that the phrase "heavenly places" refers not to a physical locality but to a realm or region of spiritual reality to which the believer has been lifted in Christ. That is to say, it speaks not of the heaven of the future but of the heaven that lies within and around the Christian here and now. Believers do indeed belong to two worlds (Phil. 3:20). Temporally they belong to the earth; but spiritually their lives are linked with Christ's, and they therefore belong to the heavenly realm.

The other phrase defining the sphere of Christian blessings is "in Christ" (vs. 3). The thought occurs no fewer than twelve times in the first fourteen verses of this Epistle. Believers are faithful in Christ (vs. 1), chosen in Him (vs. 4), receive grace in Him (vs. 6), have their redemption in Him (vs. 7), are made a heritage in Him (vs. 11, ASV), are sealed in Him (vs. 13), and so on. Here (vs. 3), where it is said that God's people are blessed in Christ, the meaning is that the blessings they experience come to them by virtue of their union with Christ. He is the great reservoir of blessing, but only those who have living connection with Him share in His benefits. To those, however, who do enjoy this vital union God gives the key to His treasures and says in effect, "Go in and take what you will."

3. *The Ground on Which They Come* (vss. 4-6). These blessings come to us in accordance with an eternal purpose of God. He "hath blessed us . . . according as [i.e., in conformity with the fact that] he hath chosen us" (vss. 3,4). The suggestion is that divine election is the source and ground of all our spiritual benefits.

If you have ever watched a surveyor checking property lines where new houses were to be built, you know how very careful he must be about where he places his transit instrument. This is because the exact point-of-beginning must be located before any surveying can be done. If the point-of-beginning is wrong, property lines will be confused, houses will be misplaced, and the courts will be flooded with people protesting the violation of their property rights. So important is this that builders refuse to begin their work until the survey is completed.

The present passage deals with the point-of-beginning in spiritual matters — both for the individual Christian and for the whole body of Christ — and traces it back to eternity, to the sovereign will of God.

The two key expressions are "hath chosen" (vs. 4) and "having predestinated" (vs. 5). Since all else in the passage revolves around these two ideas, it is absolutely necessary that we understand their meanings. "Hath chosen" means that God has chosen Christians to be His people, to be the means of carrying out His purpose in the world. The root meaning of the Greek word is "to pick out" or "select" (for oneself). It is used in various connections in the New Testament — for example, of Christ's choice of the apostles (Luke 6:13), of the early church's choice of deacons (Acts 6:5), and of the selection of official delegates by the Jerusalem conference (Acts 15:22, 25). In the present passage, where the word relates specifically to God's selection of sinners for salvation and service, there is a connotation of kindness and love.

"Having predestinated," the other focal term in our passage, translates a Greek word that literally means "to mark off in advance" (cf. Knox, "marking us out beforehand"). The idea is that of determining in advance. Other renderings are "predestined" (NIV), "destined" (TCNT, RSV, NEB), "planned" (Phillips), and "foreordained" (ASV). In the New Testament it is always used of God as determining from eternity (cf. Acts 4:28; Rom. 8:29; 30; 1 Cor. 2:7; Eph. 1:11). Probably no rigid distinction should be drawn between the choosing and the predestinating (foreordaining); they relate to the same divine act and, for all practical purposes, are identical.

Both of these expressions ("hath chosen," "having predestinated") are key terms for what is known as the doctrine of election. This doctrine, in a broad sense, may be defined as an act of choice whereby God selects an individual or group out of a larger company for a purpose or destiny that He appoints. In a more restricted sense, it is God's gracious and sovereign choice of individual sinners to be saved in and through Christ. We cannot fully comprehend the ways of God, but we may be sure that in His wisdom He knew that this was the way whereby the greatest possible blessing would eventually come to the largest number of persons.

This principle of selection has characterized God's dealings with the race from the beginning. For example, He chose Abraham from among all other men in Ur; He chose Isaac rather than Ishmael and the other sons of Abraham; He chose Jacob rather than Esau; He selected Israel over all other nations of earth and made them His "chosen people." Other examples could be cited, but these are enough to show that Paul was not teaching a new doctrine. What he does assert is that God has chosen a *new people*, and this has been done without regard to geographical or racial distinctions.

The doctrine receives great emphasis in Paul's Epistles, (cf. Rom. 8:28–11:36; 1 Thess. 1:2-10), but it is not peculiar to him. The New Testament uniformly teaches that all saving grace in time flows from divine election in eternity (cf. John 6:44,65; Acts 13:48; 1 Peter 1:1,2). The teaching is often brought in (as it is in the present passage) in contexts of praise and devotion and is intended to elicit the adoring gratitude of redeemed people.

The doctrine of election is often vigorously opposed. Sometimes this opposition arises from a misunderstanding of the doctrine. Sometimes it represents a reaction to those who have made the teaching harsh and forbidding. Often, however, the prejudice against election is an expression of imbedded conceit, for this teaching deals a crushing blow to human pride. It is indeed a leveling doctrine, stripping away all trust in flesh and bringing men to see that their only hope is the grace of God in Christ.

The KJV attaches the phrase "in love" to the thought of verse 4: "that we should be holy and without blame before him in love." Many interpreters favor placing the mark of punctuation before "in love" and construing these words with "having predestinated" (vs. 5). The RSV, for instance, has a period after the phrase "before him," then makes verse 5 read: "He destined us in love to be his sons through Jesus Christ. . . ." God's predestinating is thus seen to be no harsh and arbitrary act, but rather a gracious and merciful decree *made in love*. It is to be thought of, then, not as a blind, impersonal, and mechanical thing, but as an act of infinite goodness and wisdom. In light of this, the expression of worship and wonder that closes Paul's most detailed and profound discussion of divine election is a fitting response for all of us: "O the depth of the riches both of the wisdom and knowledge of God! how unsearchable are his judgments, and his ways past finding out!" (Rom. 11:33).

Five things about election (the divine choice) are brought out in the present passage. First, *it has its ground in Christ*.[1] God chose us "in him" (vs. 4). The thought is that apart from Christ and His foreseen work on our behalf there would have been no election and, therefore, no salvation. Since, therefore, the redemption of sinners is bound up so intimately with the person and work of God's Son, no one should think of himself as one of God's elect unless he knows himself to be in Christ. "Do not conceive," said Spurgeon, "that some decree, passed in the dark ages of eternity, will save your souls, unless you believe in Christ. Do not . . . fancy that you are to be saved without faith. . . . That

---

[1]We are here following Salmond's terminology. Calvin's interpretation, though not identical, is not radically different. He understood Paul's statement to mean that Christ is in the primary sense the "Elect" of God and that in electing Him, God chose us "in him."

is a most abominable and accursed heresy, and has ruined thousands. Lay not election as a pillow for you to sleep on, or you may be ruined" (p. 82).

Second, God's choice was made *"before the foundation of the world"* (vs. 4). That is to say, it was an eternal choice; it was made before any created thing came into being, indeed, before time began. The New Testament appears to emphasize this fact in order to bring out that God's choice is immutable, that nothing can happen in time or eternity to shake His determination to save His people. God's purposes cannot miscarry, nor can they be checkmated.

Third, God's choice was *purposeful*. This truth is brought out in two statements. The first, "that we should be holy and without blame before him" (vs. 4), expresses the purpose of divine election as to our character. God wanted us to be a certain kind of people: He wanted us to be *holy* (i.e., separated to Him); He wanted us to be *blameless*. The two words really express two sides of the same thing.

Barclay points out that the word *holy*, which speaks in this context of inner consecration, has in it "the idea of *difference* and of *separation*." His comments are significant. "A temple," he explains, "is *holy* because it is different from other buildings; a priest is *holy* because he is different from ordinary men; a [sacrificial] victim is *holy* because it is different from other animals; God is supremely *holy* because He is different from men; the Sabbath day is *holy* because it is different from other days. So, then, God chose the Christian that he should be *different* from other men" (p. 89). This difference consists in his separation, his dedication to God.

The word that is translated "without blame" is sometimes used of blamelessness in character and conduct (cf. especially the Septuagint rendering of the Psalms), but essentially it is a sacrificial term. In reference to sacrificial animals it meant "without blemish" or "without defect." In the New Testament, where the word occurs eight times, it is used in various contexts. For example, it is used of Christ, who "offered himself *without spot* to God" (Heb. 9:14) and whose blood was like that "of a lamb *without blemish*" (1 Peter 1:19); of Christians, who are to show themselves to be "children of God *without blemish*" in the midst of an evil generation (Phil. 2:15, ASV); and of the church, which as Christ's bride is one day to be presented to Him "holy and *without blemish*" (Eph. 5:27; cf. Col. 1:22; Jude 24). The root meaning of the word is "flawless." In the present passage Paul uses it to denote the stainless life that God purposes for His people to live.

The second statement of purpose is put in terms of our standing before God: "unto the adoption of children by Jesus Christ" (vs. 5). Adoption embraces more than our relationship to God as his children.

This relationship we have by the new birth. Used in the New Testament only by Paul, the Greek word for "adoption" literally means a "placing as sons." (Compare ASV, "adoption as sons"; NAB, "his adopted sons".) Once (Rom. 9:4) Paul uses it of the covenant relationship between Israel and God (cf. Exod. 4:12), but everywhere else he uses it to emphasize the privileges that belong to believers. The complete manifestation of our adoption and the full realization of its privileges are yet future (Rom. 8:23).

This adoption is further defined as "unto . . . himself" (vs. 5). The sense is that God Himself is the one to whom believers are brought into a filial relationship through adoption. Thus the phrase is practically equivalent to a possessive pronoun. Compare RSV: "He destined us in love *to be his sons* through Jesus Christ" (italics mine). The further intent of the phrase is to emphasize the glory and wonder of our adoption.

Fourth, the divine election is "*according to the good pleasure of his will*" (vs. 5). This means that the reason for God's choice, for His foreordaining us to be His children, is not to be found in us but in His own goodness and in the deliberate resolve of His own mind. F. F. Bruce explains: "It was not because He foreknew that we would believe the gospel, that He singled us out for such an honour as this. The ground must be sought exclusively in His own gracious character" (pp. 29,30). The Greek word for "good pleasure," found three times in the Gospels (Matt. 11:26; Luke 2:14; 10:21), six times in the writings of Paul (Rom. 10:1; Eph. 1:5,9; Phil. 1:15; 2:13; 2 Thess. 1:11), and nowhere else in the New Testament, suggests a gracious purpose or resolve. Salmond says that when Paul uses it of God, it is "a term of grace, expressing good pleasure as *kind* intent, *gracious* will" (p. 252). Here it directs attention to the fact that God's election is an act of His own pure goodness, of His own benevolent sovereignty. What He did, He did solely because it seemed right and good for Him to do it. "Grace," writes Simpson, "is not measured by desert, but bestowed at the option of the donor. If I give all my goods to feed the poor or ransom a crew of galley-slaves I have an undoubted right to select my beneficiaries as I think best" (p. 25).

Fifth, the ultimate[2] end of God's choice, of His foreordination of sinners, is "*the praise of the glory* (splendor) *of his grace*" (vs. 6). Just as Israel was chosen to live to God's praise (Isa. 43:21), so those who are chosen in Christ must live to the praise of the splendor of His grace. The "glory of his grace" may suggest generally grace in its gloriousness. The context shows that the reference is to the profuse outpouring of God's

---

[2]The immediate purpose has been stated in verses 4, 5: that we should be holy and blameless and that we should receive adoption into the family of God.

grace "wherein he hath made us accepted in the beloved" (vs. 6). Weymouth: "with which He has enriched us in the beloved One." The overall teaching, then, is that grace has been gloriously manifested and (because of this) is to be eternally praised. "The design of redemption," wrote Hodge, "is to exhibit the grace of God in such a conspicuous manner as to fill all hearts with wonder and all lips with praise" (p. 38).

II. AN ENUMERATION OF THE DIVINE BLESSINGS (1:7-14)

All that Paul has said in verses 3-6 constitutes a description of God's blessings to His people. Verses 7-14 enumerate some of these divine blessings.

1. *Redemption and Forgiveness* (vs. 7). "Redemption" and "the forgiveness of sins [trespasses]" (vs. 7) are joined together in such a way as to suggest the closest possible relation, but they are not identical concepts. "Redemption" denotes a release brought about by the payment of a price. Barclay calls attention to the varied uses of the word: of ransoming a slave or a prisoner of war, of releasing a man under penalty of death for some crime, of the emancipation of Israel from Egyptian bondage, and of God's rescuing His people in the time of their trouble. "In every case," he explains, "the conception is the delivering or the setting free of a man from a situation from which he himself was powerless to liberate himself, or from a penalty which he himself could never have paid" (p. 93). In Christ we have been delivered from the shackles of sin, from enslavement to Satan, and from all the misery attendant on such enslavement.

The ransom price, the means by which this release has been effected, is "his [i.e., Christ's] blood" (vs. 7). This sacrificial term calls to mind the blood of victims offered to God in the Old Testament economy. Here the word represents the death of Christ in its character as a sacrifice for sin and is a reminder to us of the infinite price God paid for our redemption.

To the idea of redemption Paul adds that of "the forgiveness of sins." The figure in the Greek word rendered by "sins" is that of a falling by the way, an offense, a trespass. Here the plural signifies the accumulation of sinful acts that were chargeable to us. "Forgiveness," a word of frequent occurrence in the New Testament, means literally "a dismissal," "a sending away" (cf. Ps. 103:11,12). The entire phrase signifies the removal of sin's guilt and the pardon of the sinner. By putting the phrase "forgiveness of sins" in grammatical apposition with the word "redemption," Paul implies that forgiveness is the central feature of our redemption.

The measure of redemption is expressed in the phrase "according to the riches of his grace" (vs. 7). God's bequests are in proportion to the abundance of His treasures. He does not give in stinted fashion but with unbounded liberality. If redemption were according to the measure of man's merit, there would be no redemption. But who can measure the wealth of God's grace?

2. *Wisdom and Prudence* (vss. 8-10). W. T. Conner used to say to his classes that Paul put emphasis on intelligence in religion. Paul teaches here that not only has God's grace brought redemption and forgiveness; it has overflowed — this is the literal meaning of the word "abound" — in the additional gifts of "wisdom and prudence" (vs. 8). Wisdom may be defined as "the knowledge that sees into the heart of things, which knows them as they really are" (Robinson, p. 307). The Greek word for "prudence" means "discernment" (TCNT, Knox), "insight" (NEB), or "practical wisdom" (Vine, p. 228). Robinson defines it as "the understanding which leads to right action" (p. 307). Wisdom here, then, is intellectual knowledge; prudence is practical understanding. One satisfies the mind; the other leads to right conduct.

In giving these gifts, Christ bestows on believers a capacity for comprehending something of God's purpose for the universe. This purpose Paul refers to as "the mystery of his [God's] will" (vs. 9). The ancients used the word *mystery* of anything hidden or secret, but in the New Testament it has a special meaning. It signifies divine truth that has now been fully made known in the gospel. The word occurs six times in Ephesians (here; 3:3,4,9; 5:32; 6:19) and twenty-one times elsewhere in the New Testament. Paul, whose writings contain the great majority of its occurrences, uses it of the thoughts and plans of God. These are hidden from human reason and comprehension and must be divinely revealed, if they are to be known at all. The TCNT renders it "hidden purpose." Perhaps the word "secret" best expresses the meaning. It is a secret, however, that has been made an *open* secret in the gospel. In Ephesians 3:3,4,9 "mystery" seems to have special reference to God's eternal purpose of including Gentiles as well as Jews in the scope of Christ's beneficent reign. In 5:32 it speaks of the spiritual union of Christ and His church. In 6:19 "mystery" is practically equated with the gospel. Here (vs. 9) it has to do with the secret of God's dealing with the world.

Verse 10 explains that the mystery (secret) with which Christians have been entrusted is nothing less than the truth about the ultimate destiny of the universe: "That . . . he might gather together in one all things in Christ." Cf. ASV, "to sum up all things in Christ." In short, then, God's purpose is "the establishment of a new order, a new creation, of which Christ shall be the acknowledged head" (Bruce, p. 32). Christ already is "head over all things to the church" (1:22); this passage declares it is God's intent that He shall be Head of a regathered, reunited universe.

"That . . . he might gather together in one" (vs. 10, KJV) translates a single Greek word that literally means "to head up" (cf. TEV) or "to sum up" (cf. ASV). The RSV renders it "to unite." The TCNT interprets it in terms of making everything "center in" Christ. The word was sometimes used in oratory for bringing all the points of a speech *to a unified conclusion.* It was also used in military affairs to describe *the heading up again* of scattered troops under the leadership of their commander. Summers sees the latter imagery in the present passage: "Paul seems to picture all . . . of God's possessions as having been scattered in the conflict with the forces of evil. It was his purpose that he would gather up all these scattered holdings and put them under one supreme captain, Jesus Christ" (p. 21).

The expression "all things" (vs. 10) is almost a technical phrase equivalent to the totality of creation. The NEB renders it "the universe." The thought is further defined by the inclusive phrases "the things in the heavens, and the things upon the earth" (vs. 10, ASV). These words do not mean that ultimately everybody is going to be saved. That interpretation is contrary to many plain teachings elsewhere in the Bible. What Paul means is that one day God's universe, into which sin has brought disorder and confusion, will be restored to harmony and unity under the headship of Jesus Christ. Ultimately everything in existence will be made to serve the sovereign purpose of God (cf. NEB). "In Christ" (vs. 10) points up the truth that the focal person in this restoration is Jesus Christ. The ultimate destiny of the universe now rests in the hands that once were nailed to the cross.[3]

The first part of verse 10 ("in the dispensation of the fulness of times") tells of the time[4] when God's purpose will be fully realized. The Greek word behind our word *dispensation* (vs. 10) is understood in different ways. Literally, it meant "management of a household." Later it came to be used of any kind of "administration" (cf. Weymouth, "government") or the working out of a "plan" (cf. RSV, NEB). The "fulness of the times" (cf. Gal. 4:4) suggests a particular point of time that completes a long prior period. The "dispensation of the fulness of the times" (ASV) speaks, then, of the carrying out (administration) of the purpose of God when the time is right (cf. NEB, TEV). The NIV translates it, ". . . to be put into effect when the times will have reached their fulfillment."

3. *A Holy Heritage* (vss. 11, 12). Three matters must be considered in interpreting these verses. First, we must notice the use of the first person pronoun in verses 11 and 12 ("we who . . . before hoped in

---

[3] A more detailed statement of the divine purpose for the world is given in 2:11–3:13.

[4] The RSV rendering ("as a plan for the fulness of time") interprets the words as a description of God's purpose.

Christ" [ASV]) and the change to the second person in verse 13 ("ye also"). The conclusion to be drawn from this is that in verses 11,12 Paul had especially in mind Jewish believers whose hope was fixed on the Messiah before He came, and "who accepted Him when He appeared either immediately (like the original disciples) or after an interval (like Paul himself)" (Bruce, pp. 34,35). The conversion of Jews who before hoped in the Messiah was thus the first stage in the realization of God's purpose to bring all the subjects of redemption into one harmonious body (cf. vs. 10). The second stage is implied in verses 13,14, where Paul shows that Gentile Christians ("ye also," vs. 13) are included in that same comprehensive purpose.

A second matter to consider is the meaning of the expression "in whom also we have obtained an inheritance" (vs. 11). This rendering suggests that God has not only imparted to believers a knowledge of His redemptive purpose but has actually made them heirs of its blessings. Understood in this manner, the passage perhaps contains an allusion to the experience of ancient Israel in obtaining an inheritance in the Promised Land. Just as each Israelite had his share of that inheritance, so each believer becomes a partaker of the heavenly inheritance Christ has secured for His people. Note the rendering of NEB: "in Christ indeed we have been given our share in the inheritance" (cf. Weymouth, Phillips). Seen in this light, the thought of the passage is quite similar to that in Colossians 1:12: "The Father . . . hath made us meet to be partakers of the inheritance of the saints in light." (See also 1 Peter 1:3-5.)

Many interpreters, however, favor the idea expressed in the ASV rendering of the verse: "in whom also we were made a heritage" (cf. TCNT, Alford, Carver, Bruce, et al.). According to this translation, the teaching is not that believers *obtain* an inheritance (though this of course is true), but rather that they themselves *become God's heritage*. The allusion is to ancient Israel's peculiar relation to God. Deuteronomy 32:9 declares that "the Lord's portion is his people; Jacob is the lot of his inheritance." Paul sees the counterpart of this idea in the present relation of believers to God. They are now God's special possession; they are His chosen people.

Verse 11b teaches that Paul and his fellow Christians from the first were "destined for this in the intention of him who in all that happens, is carrying out his own fixed purpose" (TCNT).

A third matter to be considered is God's aim in making believers His possession. This is expressed by the words "that we should be to the praise of his glory" (vs. 12). God's intention was not that believers might take pride in their position and boast of their special privileges. (Ancient Israel made this mistake in interpreting their relation to God and His purpose.) The aim is rather that, through believers, God's glory might come to be seen and adored. The TCNT: "that we should enhance his glory." Weymouth: "that we should be devoted to extolling his glorious attributes."

4. *The Gift of the Spirit* (vss. 13,14). The gift of the Spirit (cf. Acts 2:38) is to be distinguished from the gifts of the Spirit (cf. 1 Cor. 12:4ff.). The latter are special endowments bestowed by the Spirit; but the former is the Spirit Himself, given by the Father through Christ. The word *gift* does not occur in this passage, but Paul clearly had in mind the bestowal of the Spirit on believers — the final blessing in the enumeration begun at verse 7.

The main thought of verses 13,14 — the verses should be read in a modern version, such as NEB — centers around the significance of the presence of the Spirit in the life of believers. The manner in which He is referred to ("that holy Spirit of promise") is worthy of note. The Spirit is in Himself holy, and it is His mission and work to make us holy. He is called the "Spirit of promise" because His coming was the fulfillment of promise, His manifestation at Pentecost and His ministry with believers having been predicted by the prophets (cf. Joel 2:28) and reaffirmed by Christ (cf. John 14–16; Acts 1:4,5).

Two figures are used by the apostle to point up the significance of the presence of the Spirit in our lives. First, there is the figure of a seal. Believers are "sealed with" the Holy Spirit (vs. 13; cf. 4:30; 2 Cor. 1:22). The commentaries list three uses of the seal: to authenticate as genuine (cf. Neh. 9:38), to render secure (cf. Matt. 27:66), and to denote ownership (cf. Rev. 7:3). In all these senses believers are sealed, but the primary idea in the present passage appears to be the last named. Compare TCNT: "you . . . were sealed as his." Carver renders it, "stamped with the seal of God's ownership" (p. 97). Thus, when Paul affirms that Gentile believers have been sealed with the Holy Spirit, he is saying that the presence of the Spirit in their lives is the token or proof that they, as truly as Jewish believers, belong to God. (Compare this point with the thought in vss. 11,12 about being made a heritage.)

The other figure used is that of an earnest. The Holy Spirit is "the earnest of our inheritance" (vs. 14). (Note the use of the pronoun "our," by which Paul included both Jewish and Gentile believers as sharing a common experience.) The word translated "earnest," used elsewhere in the New Testament only in 2 Corinthians 1:22; 5:5, was a legal and commercial term used of a deposit, a first installment, a down payment. (The same word is used in modern Greek for an engagement ring.) The word is used here in the sense of a pledge or a guarantee.

The meaning, then, is that the presence of the Spirit in the believer's life is God's pledge that the Christian will one day enjoy in all its fullness the inheritance laid up for him.

There is a further suggestion in the use of this word. The earnest was itself a part of the purchase price, the same in kind as the full payment. The obvious inference is that our present experience of the Holy Spirit is a foretaste of the joys and blessedness of the life to come.

The phrase "until the redemption of the purchased possession" (vs. 14b) expresses one purpose of the sealing. The "purchased possession" (ASV, "God's own possession"; NEB, "what is his own") must be understood as referring to God's people (cf. 1 Peter 2:9), and the "redemption" in view is the completion of redemption. (Compare TCNT: "the full redemption of God's own people.") "The implication," writes Moulton, "is that we really belong to God, but have gone out of His possession. Through all that Christ has done, God gets us back again" (p. 85).

There is, of course, a sense in which believers already are redeemed ("bought back"); but there is another sense in which redemption is yet future. We still await "the full release to [God] of that which is his by virtue of the fact that he both made it and bought it. Fully released from all the effects of sin, his people will then be made manifest as being in very deed 'his peculiar treasure'" (Hendriksen, p. 93). But at present our redemption is incomplete. It will not be complete until we each have a resurrected and glorified body and stand before God without blemish. It is at this point that the passage at hand gives great assurance. The presence of the Spirit in our lives guarantees that what God has begun He will in due time accomplish fully.

A second and ultimate purpose in the sealing of the Spirit is expressed in the words "unto the praise of his glory" (vs. 14c). The phrase speaks of the adoring confession of God's excellence that will one day be made when the redemption of His people is consummated.

Before concluding our study of Ephesians 1:3-14, perhaps it would be well to read it again and give thought to the responses it should call forth from our hearts. Perhaps our first response should be *worship*. The whole passage, as has been pointed out, is a majestic hymn of praise to God in which the apostle sets forth those features of redemption in Christ that should elicit the gratitude of every Christian. So

> Praise, my soul, the King of heaven,
>   To His feet thy tribute bring;
> Ransomed, healed, restored, forgiven,
>   Who like thee His praise should sing?
>   Praise Him! Praise Him!
>   Praise the everlasting King!
>   — Henry Francis Lyte

Second, we should here find *encouragement*. The passage is more than a hymn of praise. It is an inspired exposition of the gracious purpose of God. Recall its leading words and phrases: "chosen," "predestinated," "his will," "his good pleasure," "the counsel of his will," and so on. All of these terms relate to the purpose of God. That purpose was formulated before time began when God chose us to be His own. It reaches beyond time to the point when the redemption of God's people will be complete. God's ultimate purpose, of course, includes the whole universe. It will not — it cannot — be frustrated. In this fact every believer can find courage and assurance as he faces a hostile world.

Finally, our response should be a renewed *dedication* to the carrying out of the will of God in our lives. Christians, like Israel in ancient times, are God's "chosen people" in the world. This is, to be sure, a position of high privilege; but it must also be interpreted in terms of mission and responsibility. We are chosen to be instruments of God for the carrying out of His purpose in the world. H. H. Rowley appropriately writes that "the Biblical doctrine of election is . . . penetrated through and through with warning. To be the elect of God is not to be His pampered favourite. It is to be challenged to a loyalty and a service and a sacrifice that knows no limits, and to feel the constraints of the Divine love to such a degree that no response can seem adequate and no service worthy" (p. 168).

FOR FURTHER STUDY

1. Read Ephesians 1:10 in several versions. Write out in your own words what you think it means. Underline the verse and print "KEY VERSE" in the margin of your study Bible.

2. Read Ephesians in a translation you have not used before. Mark in your Bible the occurrences of the word *all*.

3. Using a concordance, study passages in which some of the key words of Ephesians 1:3-14 are found. Examples of such words are "choose," "foreordain," "redemption," "inheritance," "salvation," "earnest," and "possession."

4. H. C. G. Moule speaks of "the infinite Free-Will of God" as being "even more sacred than the free-will of man." Evaluate his statement.

5. For further help on the doctrine of election, secure J. I. Packer's *Evangelism and the Sovereignty of God* (Downer's Grove, Ill.: Inter-Varsity Press, 1961). A helpful chapter may also be found in W. T. Conner's *The Gospel of Redemption* (Nashville: Broadman Press, 1943).

CHAPTER 4

The Resources of God's New People: A Prayer

(Ephesians 1:15-23)

Many necessary and worthwhile endeavors compete for the Christian's time and energy, but without doubt prayer is the most important thing that ever engages his attention. It nurtures the soul, refines the character, promotes spiritual growth, and gives fortitude for victorious Christian living. The day of judgment will likely show that those who have done the most to advance God's cause in the world have been persons who made prayer a large factor in their lives. It is unquestionably the mightiest weapon that one can wield in the struggle against evil.

A person's prayers are the mirror of his inner life. They reflect the depth of his emotions, the tenderness of his affection, the breadth of his sympathies, and the sincerity of his devotion. Moreover, a person's prayers are an index to his sense of values. They reveal the things he considers to be really important.

Paul's prayers are in some respects the high-water mark of his Epistles. Blaikie writes of them: "They are very short, but wonderfully deep and comprehensive; very rich and sublime in aspiration; powerful in their pleas, whether expressed or implied; and exhaustive in the range of blessings which they implore" (p. 6). Nowhere else, Maclaren observes, "do Paul's words come more winged and fast, or his spirit glow with greater fervour of affection and holy desire than in his petitions for his friends" (p. 52): With some people prayer appears to be an unpleasant duty; with Paul it was obviously a supreme joy.

This particular prayer is by no means an ordinary one, for it is replete with profound spiritual truth. In fact, this passage is so full of instruction that it is difficult to know where the prayer ends and the distinctly didactic portion of the Epistle begins. Beare sees 1:15–2:10 as all a part of the prayer. Other interpreters arbitrarily make the break at the end of verse 19. We prefer to retain verses 15-23 as a unit, and, while there is not a sharp break at the end of verse 23, think it best to construe 2:1-10 as introducing a new division. Our discussion focuses on (1) the

31

occasion for the prayer (vs. 15), (2) the substance of the prayer (vss. 16-19a), and (3) the expansion of the prayer (vss. 19b-23).

I. The Occasion for the Prayer (1:15)

Two things are mentioned as moving the apostle to prayer on behalf of the Christians to whom he wrote this letter. The first was the amazing display of divine grace in their lives. This idea is suggested by the word "wherefore" (vs. 15), which points back in a general way to the great truths of verses 13, 14, where Paul has set out the signal manifestation of God's grace in sealing the Gentile believers with the Holy Spirit. Paul apparently believed that present attainments in grace not only give occasion for gratitude but also afford encouragement to expect that yet greater blessings may be had from the hand of God.

The second occasion for this prayer is brought out in the words "after I heard of your faith in the Lord Jesus, and love unto all the saints" (vs. 15). "Faith" and "love," two great words that denote the leading graces of Christian character, sum up the experience of the Asian Christians. Faith, which essentially means "trust," may here refer either to the readers' initial believing acceptance of the gospel or to their continuing experience of constancy and fidelity. (The same word is used in Galatians 5:22, where it designates a fruit of the Spirit, rendered "faithfulness" in RSV.) But, whether faith or faithfulness, it operates "in Christ Jesus." The Greek word for love (agape)[1] denotes caring love, love that counts no sacrifice too great for the one loved. Such was the attitude of Paul's readers toward "all the saints" (i.e., the people of God).

Some scholars have inferred from the phrase "after I heard" that Paul had had no personal acquaintance with the readers of this letter and that they therefore could not have been the Ephesians, among whom he had lived for three years and of whose conversion he had personal acquaintance. This interpretation, however, appears to read too much into the words. And, as explained above, the reference may not be to the initial experience of conversion at all. It had been some years since the apostle had been in Ephesus, and the "having heard" probably refers to what he had heard in the interval.

II. The Substance of the Prayer (1:16-19a)

Paul's prayer reveals something of his deep concern for his readers and of his great joy in the work of grace they had experienced. It has,

---

[1]The best manuscripts do not contain the word for "love"; Beare, Robertson, and others think it should be omitted in translation. Without it, however, the construction is difficult and awkward. Phillips renders it: ". . . this faith of yours in the Lord Jesus and the practical way in which you are expressing it toward fellow Christians" (cf. ASV). The RSV, NEB, NIV, TEV, and others retain the word *love* in spite of weak manuscript support.

therefore, two main themes: thanksgiving (vs. 16) and intercession (vss. 17-19a)

1. *Thanksgiving* (vs. 16). Paul's prayer is, first, one of thanksgiving. He was not unmindful of moral and spiritual deficiencies in those whom he served, but he was the kind of man who was able also to recognize the good in them.

The word for "give thanks" (vs. 16) is characteristically Pauline, being found in his writings twenty-six times. In his letter to the Romans, for example, he thanks God that their "faith is spoken of throughout the whole world" (1:8). In 1 Corinthians he writes of his gratitude "for the grace of God which was given you in Christ Jesus" (1:4, ASV). He thanks God "upon every remembrance of" the Philippians (Phil. 1:3). And in his second letter to the Thessalonians he writes, "We are bound to give thanks to God always for you" (1:3). Blaikie speaks of the frequency of Paul's thanksgiving as "indicating the prevalence in him of a bright, joyous state of mind." Then he adds: "Constantly to recognize God's goodness in the past begets a larger expectation of it in the future" (p. 6).

Three things may be said about the thanksgiving of Paul as expressed in the present passage. First, that for which he is especially grateful is the good news of the faith and love of the readers. Second, his gratitude is constant and continual ("I cease not"). Third, it is addressed to God. Thus does the apostle recognize that God is the true fountain of all that is good in His people.

2. *Petition* (vss. 17-19a). This prayer is mainly one of petition or intercession. The burden of it is "that the God of our Lord Jesus Christ, the Father of glory, may give unto you the spirit of wisdom and revelation . . . that ye may know . . ." (vss. 17,18).

Observe that the person to whom the prayer is addressed is designated as "the God of our Lord Jesus Christ, the Father of glory." From this sublime title we learn that Paul's approach to God had nothing of thoughtless and irreverent familiarity about it. And we would do well to imitate him in this respect. When we go to God in prayer, there ought to be a profound reverence, a sense of deep and inexpressible wonder. Furthermore, the title reveals something of the encouragement Paul found to pray. To think of God as "the God of our Lord Jesus Christ" is to recall His nearness, to be reminded that in praying to Him we approach a "throne of grace."

To speak of God as "the God of our Lord Jesus Christ" (cf. 1:3) in no sense detracts from the uniqueness of Christ. God is the God of Christ in the sense that He is the God whose work Christ came to perform and by whom Christ was sent into the world. He was truly man and as such He "had God for His God as we have Him for our God" (Salmond, p. 245). To speak of God as "the Father of glory" is to say that He is the Father who possesses glory (splendor), the Father of whom glory (splendor) is a characteristic feature (cf. NIV, which renders it "glorious Father").

The prayer takes the form of a single definite request: that "the Father . . . may give unto you the spirit of wisdom and revelation" (vs. 17). And this request is for a definite end: "that ye may know . . ." (vs. 18).

The "spirit of wisdom" is often interpreted as an attitude of mind, as when we speak of a spirit of meekness or of courage. Understood in this fashion, the words express a desire of the apostle that his readers may have an attitude of mind, a spiritual disposition, by which they will be able to comprehend divine truth. This interpretation is apparently the one the translators of the KJV followed, for the word "spirit" is not capitalized. However, it should probably be capitalized (cf. NIV) and understood as a reference to the Holy Spirit.[2] If such be done, the verse is seen as a prayer for the readers to experience to the fullest degree the blessed ministry of the Spirit — particularly in his capacity as "Spirit of wisdom and revelation." Apart from the illumination produced by this ministry of the Spirit there can be no understanding of divine truth.

Observe that the knowledge of which Paul speaks is not simply a knowledge of things or facts; it is knowledge — the Greek word denotes accurate, thorough, full knowledge[3] — which concerns God ("in the knowledge of *him*," vs. 17). Such knowledge requires that "the eyes of . . . [one's] understanding" be "enlightened" (vs. 18). With these words the apostle explains the last part of verse 17. That is, to have the Spirit of wisdom and revelation is to have the eyes of one's understanding ("heart," ASV, RSV, NIV, et al.) enlightened. In Paul's writings, "heart" stands for the whole inner man. Its use here reminds us that the illumination needed is inward and spiritual.

"That ye may know" (vs. 18) introduces the three specific elements of knowledge that Paul desires his readers to possess: "the hope of his calling" (vs. 18), "the riches of the glory of his inheritance in the saints" (vs. 18), and "the exceeding greatness of his power to us-ward who believe" (vs. 19). Note that it is *God's* calling, *God's* inheritance, and *God's* power. But more specifically, it is the *hope* of His calling, the *glory* of His inheritance, and the *greatness* of His power that Paul wants the readers to grasp and appreciate.

(1) The hope of his calling (vs. 18). The ancient world was a world

---

[2]Blaikie, following Alford, thinks that "spirit" here is neither exclusively the Holy Spirit nor the spirit of man, but "the complex idea of the spirit of man dwelt in and moved by the Spirit of God" (p. 6).

[3]This is perhaps why NIV translates, "so that you may know him *better*" (italics mine).

without hope (Eph. 2:12). A current saying was: "Not to be born at all —
that is by far the best fortune; the second best is to die as soon as one is
born." But all of this was changed for Christians. The reception of Christ
and the knowledge of His resurrection opened up for them a new world
of unexpected wonder and glory. The future was no longer something to
be dreaded or even to be accepted with resignation. It could now be
faced with eager anticipation and assurance.

The word *hope* is used in two different ways in the Scriptures. It
may be used *objectively* for the things hoped for. (Col. 1:5 is an example:
"the hope which is laid up for you in heaven.") If taken in this sense,
hope speaks here of the outcome or issue of redemption, the ultimate
consummation of the purpose of God as it respects His people. In
praying that his readers may "know" this hope, Paul is asking not only
that they may know what it really and essentially is but that they may
understand something of its compass and scope. It is possible that this
interpretation is the one to be given in this passage.

Sometimes, however, "hope" is used in a *subjective* sense, that is,
of an expectant attitude — the absolute certainty of future bliss. For
example, note 1 Peter 1:13: "Set your hope perfectly on the grace that is
to be brought unto you at the revelation of Jesus Christ" (ASV). The same
meaning is to be given to the word in Romans 5:2: "We rejoice in hope of
the glory of God" (ASV). To "know" hope in this sense is to have conscious
experience of it. Paul therefore was praying that his readers, who
already had this hope in their hearts, might come to experience its
power in ever-increasing measure.

It is quite possible that there is in this passage a blending of both the
subjective and the objective ideas. This view is held by Scroggie, who
says that Paul's prayer is "that we may know in happy experience the
expectation which God's saving calling of us has begotten in our souls;
and that we may know also what that calling has secured for us, and
reserves for us in the heavenly life which awaits us" (p. 52).

The hope of the Christian springs from the "calling" of God. This
calling is God's in the sense that it is He who extends it to us (cf. NIV). A
favorite word with Paul, "calling" refers not merely to a general invita-
tion to salvation but to the effectual call of God that actually issues in
conversion. This is the uniform meaning of the word in Paul's writings, for the called of God, in his view, are those who have obeyed
God's summons and have been made believers in Christ (cf. Rom.
8:28-30).

(2) "The riches of the glory of his inheritance in the saints" (vs. 18).
These words also are capable of more than one interpretation. The main
question is whether the reference is to *God's* inheritance in the saints or
to the *saints'* inheritance in God. The former view is very widely held

and has much to commend it. On the surface it appears to be the more obvious interpretation. The text does not speak of our inheritance in God, but of "his inheritance in the saints." And verses 11 ("we were made a heritage," ASV) and 14 ("the purchased possession") have already made reference to this idea.

Viewed in this manner, the text expresses Paul's desire that believers may know how precious they are to God and what God expects of and from them. He has taken them to be His everlasting portion and has made them trophies of His grace and power. Their treasure is in God, and in a very true sense His treasure is in them. Bruce, who subscribes to this interpretation, points out that "we can scarcely realize what it must mean to God to see His purpose complete, to see creatures of His hand, sinners redeemed by His grace, reflecting His own glory" (p. 40).

Many, however, feel constrained to interpret the passage as a reference to the saints' inheritance in God. One argument is that it is easy to conceive of our inheritance in God as rich in glory, but difficult to think of the heritage He has in us in this way. Accordingly, it is felt that the inheritance refers to the future glory of believers, the pronoun "his" being understood to denote origin. The inheritance is "his," then, in the sense that it originates in God and is given by Him to His people. "In the saints" must then refer to the manner in which the inheritance is distributed among them, with an allusion to the partitioning of the Promised Land among the Israelites of old.

One other matter should be observed here. Paul's request was not simply that his readers might have knowledge of their inheritance. His prayer was that they might know "the riches of the glory" of it. That is to say, he was anxious for the Ephesians to appreciate fully the magnificence and the splendor of their inheritance in Christ. The accumulation of descriptive words shows that Paul was laboring to convey the sense of wonder that he himself felt in contemplating it.

(3) "The exceeding greatness of his power" (vs. 19a). The "call" refers to the past; the "inheritance" points to the future; the "power" concerns the present, and suggests the limitless resources available to God's people. (Cf. NEB, "how vast the resources of his power open to us who trust in him.") Realizing that the very thought of the riches of the glorious inheritance held out for Christians may tend to quench rather than stimulate hope of entering into it, Paul encourages his readers by reminding them of the surpassing greatness of God's power at work in them. "The whole energy of the divine Being is turned on to our feeble, languid nature, vivifying, purifying, and transforming it, making it wonderfully active where all was feebleness before, as the turning on of steam wakens up a whole mass of inert machinery" (Blaikie, p. 7). It is

this operative power that brings the fulfillment of the hope and makes possible the realization of the inheritance.

III. THE EXPANSION OF THE PRAYER (1:19b-23)

Verses 19b-23 continue Paul's great prayer, but the tone changes from petition to adoration and praise, and the whole is expanded and enlarged so as to take on a didactic character. The passage consists of a description of the exaltation and glory of Jesus Christ, and shows that the divine power at work in believers (cf. vs. 19a) is the same as that which God put forth in raising Christ from the dead and exalting Him to the throne of the universe.

1. *The Measure of God's Power* (vs. 19b). Paul's concern was not simply that the readers might *know* the power of God; he wanted them to know "the exceeding greatness" of it. Something of the superlative strength of that power is brought out by the remarkable accumulation of terms: "exceeding greatness," "power" (Greek, *dunamis*), "working" (Greek, *energeia*), "strength" (Greek, *kratos*), "might" (Greek, *ischus*). The heaping up of words suggests the idea of power the very telling of which exhausts the resources of language and finally defies description.

2. *The Supreme Demonstration of God's Power* (vss. 20-23). Even if this power is beyond description, Paul can nonetheless point to the supreme demonstration of it in the person of Christ. It is described as the "working of the strength" of God's might" which he wrought in Christ, when he raised him from the dead" (vss. 19,20, ASV). God's power at work in believers, then, is none other than resurrection power (Cf. Phil. 3:10). It is the power that raised Christ from the dead, seated Him at God's right hand, and gave Him supremacy over all the universe. What tremendous encouragement this truth should give to believers! The power available to us in daily living is not to be conceived of as a tiny brook, barely meeting the demands made on it. It is like a surging river, driving before itself all the obstacles it may encounter.

In developing this theme, Paul makes three far-reaching affirmations about what God has done in and for Christ. The pivotal expressions are these: "He raised . . . and made him to sit" (vs. 20, ASV); "he put . . . in subjection" (vs. 22a, ASV); and "gave him to be head" (vs. 22b, ASV).

(1) The resurrection and exaltation of Christ (vss. 20,21). The raising of Christ from the dead and His exaltation to the right hand of God are attributed specifically to the exertion of God's mighty power. ("Raised" and "set" are, in the Greek, participles modifying the finite verb, "he wrought."[4]) The two things (the raising from the dead and

---

[4]"Wrought" translates a verb (*energeken*) that is cognate with the noun for "working"

the seating at God's right hand) are really two stages of one epochal event.

The resurrection of Christ, the fact of which was continuously and joyously proclaimed by the apostles, is a matter of supreme importance. It authenticated the Lord's ministry, sealed His redemptive work, marked the beginning of His glorification, and was a public attestation of the Father's acceptance of His sacrifice. Moreover, it provides the dynamic, the power, for Christian living and is the pattern and pledge of the believer's resurrection. Since Christ has "become the firstfruits of them that slept" (1 Cor. 15:20), we therefore confidently await the hour when He "shall fashion anew the body of our humiliation, that it may be conformed to the body of his glory" (Phil. 3:21, ASV).

Having raised Christ from the dead, God further exhibited His power by causing Him to sit "at his own right hand" (vss: 20, 21). These words, which allude to Psalm 110:1, speak of the enthronement of Christ. The "right hand" of God is a figurative expression for the place of supreme privilege and authority. Christ therefore has been given the highest honor and authority in the universe (cf. Matt. 28:18).

The local sense of "heavenly places" is more prominent here than in Ephesians 1:3, for Christ did literally and bodily ascend to heaven. But we need not make the phrase exclusively local. Along with heaven itself, it may also include the whole region of spiritual things over which Christ rules. (See the discussion of 1:3.)

Verse 21 is an expansion of Paul's statement about the exaltation of Christ. More precisely, it describes the extent of Christ's sovereign authority. He has been enthroned, the apostle writes, "far above all rule, and authority, and power, and dominion, and every name that is named"[5] (vs. 21, ASV). Likely, the words refer to various ranks and orders of celestial greatness among angelic beings, but it is not necessary to draw fine lines of distinction between the terms. Brought together as they are, they have a cumulative effect and tellingly express the unique supremacy and sovereign power of Jesus Christ. Whatever kinds of spiritual rulership there may be and whatever names they may bear, they are not even remotely comparable to Him to whom God has given "the name which is above every name" (Phil. 2:9).

This sovereign and unshared supremacy of Christ holds true "not only in this world [age], but also in that which is to come" (vs. 21). Above all grades of rulership, real or imagined, good or evil, present or future,

---

(energeia) in verse 19. The tense is perfect, pointing "to the raising of Christ from the dead not as an isolated event of past history, but as a divine accomplishment which is a present guarantee of God's life-giving power" (Beare, p. 633).

[5]For "every name that is named" the NIV reads "every title that can be given."

God has exalted and enthroned the crucified and risen Christ.

(2) The universal dominion of Christ (vs. 22). Verse 22 sums up what has already been said about Christ's exaltation, but the description it gives is even more sweeping. It makes clear that Christ's exaltation carries with it sovereign lordship over *all* creation. The head that was once crowned with thorns now wears the diadem of universal dominion. Two great deeds of God are in view: (a) He wrought His power in raising and exalting Christ (vss. 20, 21) and (b) He subjected all things to Him (vs. 22).[6]

This dominion of Christ is affirmed in words drawn from Psalm 8:6 (cf. Heb. 2:8, where the same words are quoted). In the psalm they speak of man and the dominion God intended him to have. Here, with the suggestion that God's ideal for man has been realized in Christ, they graphically depict the placing of all things under His sovereign lordship. The reference to "all things" being "put under" Christ's feet means that all things are arranged under Him, subordinated to Him. The words imply absolute subjection, but their complete fulfillment, as brought out in 1 Corinthians 15:27, will not come until death itself is destroyed. Christ's present enthronement at God's right hand, however, is the pledge that such will come to pass.

(3) The headship of Christ over the church (vss. 22,23). God has established a unique relationship between Christ and the church. He "gave him to be head over all things to the church" (asv). There are two lines of interpretation of this statement. One takes the verb "gave" quite literally and construes "to the church" with it. Accordingly, Christ is seen as in some sense *God's gift to the church* (cf. Lenski, Beare). It is an astounding statement, and a concept that staggers the imagination. This exalted, sovereign Christ, a gracious gift of God to His redeemed people — what a stupendous Gift!

Those who advocate this interpretation further suggest that God gave Christ to the church in a certain capacity. The verse might be translated, "He gave him, *as head over all things,* to the church." Thus understood, "head over all things" repeats the substance of "hath put all things under his feet" and simply restates the thought of Christ's absolute and supreme dominion over all the universe. Blaikie, a proponent of this view, writes, "The exaltation of Christ is not merely an honour conferred on himself, but has also a definite practical purpose; it is for the benefit of the Church. . . . The gift of Christ to the Church is the gift of One who has sovereign authority over all things" (p. 8).

In this interpretation the headship of Christ over the church is not

---

[6]As was pointed out earlier in our discussion, "raised" and "set" (vs. 20) are participles qualifying the expression "he wrought" (vs. 20). But "hath put" (vs. 22) is a verb in finite form, co-ordinate with "wrought" (vs. 20).

explicitly stated. The idea is implied, however, by the statements that follow, especially in the reference to the church as "his body" (vs. 23).

The other line of interpretation attaches to the verb "gave" the somewhat weakened meaning of "appointed." Furthermore, those who advocate this view construe the words "head over all things" more intimately with "to the church," and interpret these latter words in the sense of "with reference to the church." Thus God "gave [appointed] him to be head over all things [i.e., supreme head] with reference to the church" (cf. NEB, NIV). In this view there is an explicit, not simply an implied, teaching of the headship of Christ over the church. This headship, however, is still admittedly a part of the larger concept of the universal dominion of Christ set forth in the preceding verses.

Three things are emphasized in the figure of Christ's headship over the church: First, He has supreme *authority* over the church; He guides, governs, and controls it. To Him the church is wholly responsible. Second, a vital *union* exists between Christ and His church, a union as close and real as that of head and body. The relationship of the two is therefore intimate, tender, and indissoluble. Third, the church is completely *dependent* upon Christ. From Him it derives its life, its power, and all else required for its existence.

Though the New Testament gives great prominence to the church, it does not in so many words define it. The basic concept is that of a company or fellowship of people belonging to Christ and acknowledging His rulership over their lives.

The Greek word translated "church" (*ekklesia*) was used by the ancients of a public assembly or meeting summoned by a herald. In the Greek translation of the Old Testament the term is sometimes used for the congregation of the Israelites, especially when assembled before God for religious purposes.

In the New Testament by far the most frequent use of *ekklesia* is for a local and organized company of believers joined together for worship, service, and fellowship — for example, the "church of the Thessalonians" (1 Thess. 1:1), the "churches of Galatia" (Gal. 1:2), and so on. Indeed, out of a total of one hundred fifteen occurrences of the word *church*, at least ninety to a hundred of them must be interpreted in a local sense. In Ephesians, however, the term seems not to be confined to a local assembly but to be given its most comprehensive and general sense. It goes beyond the concept of a concrete institution or outward, visible organization to that of a great spiritual fellowship including all of the redeemed.

The concept of the church permeates the entire book of Ephesians, though the word itself is found in only three of its six chapters (here, ch. 3, and ch. 5). In 3:10 the church is referred to as the means by which celestial beings learn of "the manifold wisdom of God." In 3:21 glory is to redound to God "in the church . . . throughout all áges, world without end." In the fifth chapter, where the word is used six times (vss. 23,24,25,27,29,32), the church is described as the bride of Christ, loved by Him, redeemed by Him, and subject to Him.

Two profound statements are made about the church in verse 23 of the present passage. First, it is said to be "his [Christ's] body." By speaking of the community of the redeemed in this fashion emphasis is placed on the idea of the intimate union of Christ and His people. Together they constitute one organism, each, in a sense, being incomplete without the other. Moreover, there may be the added suggestion that believers exist not simply to enjoy a mystic union with Christ but to be of practical service to Him. He, as their Head, is the source of their life and power; and they, as His body, are the means by which He carries out His work in the world.

Second, the church is said to be "the fulness of him that filleth all in all."[7] The thought seems to be, according to some, that the church as Christ's body is filled by Him. This is the view of Salmond, who explains it to mean that the church is "pervaded by His presence, animated by His life, filled with His gifts and energies and graces" (p. 282). It thereby receives from Christ all that it requires for the realization of its calling and the accomplishment of its mission. Others think that the phrase continues the figure of the body and therefore take it to mean that the church fills Christ. That is to say, the church as Christ's body is the complement of Him. It is the sphere in which He exercises His messianic functions, the instrument by which He manifests His power and carries out His purposes. He (the Head) and the church (His body) form an organic unity, and each, in a sense, is incomplete without the other. This, of course, does not mean that Christ is dependent on the church for His existence as the church is dependent on Him. Paul was thinking of Him "not in the absoluteness of his divine nature, but in the contingent manifestation of him in his function as Messiah. The Messiah, regardless of his nature, cannot function as Messiah in the void; he must have as his counterpart the people which he is to deliver and rule" (Beare, p. 637).

SUMMARY

The practical lessons to be gained from a study of these verses are many. Three may be mentioned: First, the passage points up the need for clear thinking about the content and meaning of our faith. Recall the

---

[7]A few scholars see this phrase as a description of Christ. He, it is said, is the fullness of God, who fills all in all (cf. Col. 1:19; 2:9). Most interpreters, however, feel that the context requires the word *fullness* to be seen as a description of the church.

many words in it that speak of mental activity: "wisdom," "knowledge," "understanding," "enlightened," "know." At a time when there is an unparalleled explosion of knowledge in so many areas, Christians must not be guilty of shoddy thinking about divine truth.

Second, the study of this passage calls for a personal appropriation of the spiritual realities it unfolds. The hope, the inheritance, and the power God gives must be more than mere facts stored away in our minds. They must be experienced in such a way that we live in their strength day by day.

Third, the crowning truth of this passage concerns the headship of Christ over the church. In a practical way this means that every church is subject to Christ's authority and every action of the church should therefore be an expression of His will. Every worship service should be hallowed by a sense of Christ's glorious presence, and every response of our hearts should be marked by submission to His will, dedication to His purposes, and praise of His grace and glory.

For Further Study

1. Read again the prayer of Ephesians 1:15-23 in a modern translation. As you read, seek to make it a genuine experience of prayer for yourself.

2. Using a concordance, study passages in which the words "hope," "calling," "inheritance," "glory," "power," etc., occur.

3. Read an article on "Ascension" in a Bible dictionary.

4. Read Spurgeon's sermon "The Mighty Power Which Creates and Sustains Faith" in *The Treasury of the Bible: New Testament*.

CHAPTER 5

The Formation of God's New People:
By the Quickening of Individuals Dead in Sin

(Ephesians 2:1-10)

The God of the Bible is a God of purpose. He does not act aimlessly. All that He has ever done or ever will do is the expression of deliberate design on His part. The opening chapter of Ephesians has pointed up the all-embracing scope of the divine purpose. It includes the whole universe and reaches from eternity to eternity. Such expressions as "the will of God" (1:1), "predestinated" (1:5,11), "hath purposed" (1:4), and "the counsel of his own will" (1:11) have abounded. In a specific way the first chapter has taken us back to the counsels of God and let us see how He purposed from eternity to call out in Christ a people for Himself — a new, redeemed humanity. This new, redeemed humanity has Christ for its Head, and it constitutes His body.

The second chapter of Ephesians tells how, in time, God is actually creating this redeemed society. Two things are stressed: (1) The new humanity is created by the spiritual resurrection of believers (vss. 1-10). From this it may be seen that God's concern is not simply for the race *en masse.* His intention takes account of each individual believer. He has a purpose, a goal, and an end in view in saving each one. (2) The creation of this new humanity involves the uniting of believing Jews and believing Gentiles into one spiritual body (vss. 11-22).

Ephesians 2:1-10 is closely connected with the concluding verses of chapter 1. The latter verses (1:20-23) declare that God's power raised Christ from the dead and gave Him universal dominion. The present passage (2:1-10) shows that the same power is at work in raising believers from the death of sin and lifting them to the "heavenly places" in Christ. (Observe the opening words of verse 1: "And you." The Greek might be rendered, "You also," thus making even clearer the intimate connection of 2:1-10 with the closing verses of chapter 1.)

In the Greek text the first seven verses of chapter 2 are one long and involved sentence. The main verb (translated "hath quickened") is not reached until verse 5. (For the sake of clarity, most English translations insert in verse 1 the words "hath quickened" or "made alive," but there is no equivalent for them in the Greek of verse 1. Note italics of KJV.) The two leading ideas are: "You . . . were dead" (vs. 1), and "God . . . hath quickened" (vss. 4,5). The whole paragraph is a sort of spiritual biography describing what believers once were apart from Christ (vss. 1-3), what they have become in Christ (vss. 4-6), and God's purpose in effecting this remarkable transformation (vss. 7-10).

I. THE STATE BEFORE CONVERSION (2:1-3)

Paul sets forth the pre-Christian state of his readers in order to emphasize the magnitude of both the power and the mercy they have experienced. The description of their former life thus becomes a sort of foil against which the amazing power and grace of God stand out in brilliant relief. Three frightening indictments are made: They were dead (vs. 1); they were enslaved to evil (vss. 2,3a); they were objects of divine wrath (vs. 3b).[1]

1. *Deadness* (vs. 1). Paul begins this spiritual biography by reminding the Ephesians that once they were alive to the lures of sin, but dead to God. The idea of deadness suggests alienation from God, the source of life, and emphasizes the sinner's helplessness to save himself. The rendering of KJV ("in trespasses and sins"; cf. NEB) represents trespasses and sins as the element or realm in which the death is experienced. The reading of ASV, "through your trespasses and sins," assigns the cause of the deadness. It is as though the whole world were one vast graveyard and every gravestone had the same inscription: "Dead through sin." The manifestations of this death are seen in the moral decay, the spiritual blindness, and the indifference to the things of God that characterize the unregenerate. If Paul was correct in his assessment of the unregenerate state (and we are convinced that he was), then it is apparent that the difference between a Christian and a non-Christian is as great as the difference between a living person and a corpse.

The word for "trespasses" represents sin as a fall, a false step, an offense. It suggests losing one's way or straying from the right road. The word for "sin," which is the more common New Testament term, represents sin as a missing the mark. It suggests the picture of a person shooting at a target and falling short of it. There is perhaps little difference here in the essential meaning of the two words. They are used together as a comprehensive description of every kind of sin that characterizes the unconverted life. Both make it clear that man has failed to measure up to God's standard of right.

---

[1]Though written of people belonging to an ancient pagan society, the same charges may be justly made against all who are outside of Jesus Christ. Deadness, enslavement, and subjection to divine wrath are the marks of a Christless life in any age.

2. *Enslavement to Evil* (vss. 2,3a). Verses 2,3a contain two leading statements, one specifically naming the Gentile readers of this letter ("ye," vs. 2), the other more general and including Paul and his fellow Jews ("we all," vs. 3). Within these two statements, however, there are four separate ideas. They vividly depict a state of moral degradation and spiritual enslavement.

(1) Walking in trespasses and sins (vs. 2a). The readers are reminded that "in time past" they had "walked" in trespasses and sins. The word "walk" — a common one in the New Testament — is here used ethically for the walk of life, the whole of one's manner of living. It is a Hebraism originally associated with the figure of life as a path that one treads. Beare says that "the metaphorical sense is seldom in evidence" in New Testament usage, but the word always retains "its reference to the moral and spiritual quality of life" (p. 639). Trespasses and sins are thought of as forming the very atmosphere in which these people once lived (cf. Rom. 1:18-32).

(2) Conforming to the standards of the world (vs. 2b). The standard to which the readers' lives had conformed prior to their conversion is expressed in the words "according to the course [age] of this world" (vs. 2). The phrase is practically equivalent to what we mean when we speak of "the worldly fashion of the day" (cf. NEB, "the evil ways of this present age"; Phillips, "this world's ideas of living"). To live in this manner is to conform to the world's shifting standards of right and wrong, to be swept up in its pleasures and its practices.

(3) Ruled over by Satan (vs. 2c). In their pre-Christian life the readers were under the power and dominion of Satan, who is here called the "prince [ruler] of [over] the power [authority] of the air" (vs. 2). "Their life was determined and shaped by the master of all evil, the supreme ruler of all the powers of wickedness" (Salmond, p. 284). This terrible picture is tragically true of the spiritual bondage of all who are strangers to God's grace in Christ.

The "power of the air" speaks of the totality of evil powers over whom Satan rules as prince. Some interpreters understand the "air" to refer to the atmosphere about us, the idea being that it is the realm of Satan's authority. Beare, a proponent of this view, explains that the phrase is not intended to limit Satan's activity to the air; "the point must be rather to emphasize how closely the power of evil crowds in upon human life, impregnating the very atmosphere" (p. 640). Others (e.g., Hodge) see in the word an allusion not to the abode of these evil powers but to their nature. They are "of the air" in that they do not belong to the earth; they do not have a corporeal nature. They are superhuman, spiritual beings ruled over by Satan (cf. Eph. 6:12, ASV).

There is a question as to the exact grammatical connection of the words "the spirit that now worketh in the children of disobedience" (vs. 2). The KJV, for example, puts them in apposition with "prince" and thus takes them to be an additional description of Satan. (The same interpretation is reflected in the renderings of RSV and NEB.) Viewed in this manner, the passage teaches that Satan not only fills the *air* about men but is active *within* them. Others make the words dependent on "prince," and see them as denoting another realm that Satan rules over. (This reading of the text requires that a word such as "of" be placed before the words "the spirit" [cf. ASV and NASB.) The meaning then is: Satan is the prince of the power of the air; he is also the prince or ruler of the spirit that now works in the children of disobedience. This "spirit" may be understood as what we mean when we speak of the spirit of the age. Thus interpreted, Paul is saying that the spirit of the age (the evil principle) that is at work in unbelievers is ruled over and controlled by the prince of evil. Some contrast may be intended between the evil spirit at work in non-Christians and the Holy Spirit at work in Christians.

"Children of . . ." is a Hebraic form of expression used to describe or characterize. (Cf. "children of this world" [Luke 16:8; 20:34]; "children of light" [1 Thess. 5:5].) The "children of disobedience," therefore, are people whose nature and essential character is disobedience. The word translated "disobedience" is always used in the Bible of disobedience toward God. Here it depicts unregenerate man as in rebellion against the God who made him (cf. NEB).

(4) At the mercy of their passions (vs. 3a). Verse 2 describes the manner in which Paul's Gentile readers had "walked" in their pre-Christian lives. In verse 3 he includes himself and his fellow Jews in his indictment, for Gentiles were not the only people who had lived in accordance with the standards of the "children of disobedience." Among them "we all," Jewish as well as Gentile believers, "once lived" (vs. 3, ASV). This statement was a tremendous admission for a Jew, once a proud Pharisee, to make; but "Paul seldom misses the opportunity of declaring the universal sinfulness of men, the dire level of corruptness on which all stood, however they differed in race or privilege (Salmond, p. 285).

Paul spells out his point very clearly. All men, prior to the work of redeeming grace in their hearts, live "in the lusts of . . . their flesh" (vs. 3). This means that the unregenerate are at the mercy of their passions. Beare says the thought is "of conduct swayed by irrational impulses; lacking any considered governing behavior" (p. 641).

The Greek word for "lusts," though not always having a bad connotation, in the present passage speaks of a desire for what is forbidden. The word "flesh" should not be understood in a strictly physical sense; flesh as representing the material side of our being is not necessarily bad. However, sin has infected the flesh, and since this is so, the word "flesh" as used by Paul normally stands for the unregenerate nature, "the whole moral temperament, as disposed to evil and hostile to the leadings of the Spirit of God" (Beare, p. 641). The TCNT translates it "earthly nature"; Weymouth, "lower nature." It signifies man as apart from God and is very fairly represented by the word "self" as used in popular religious language.

Jews and Gentiles alike, prior to meeting God in Christ, habitually carry out "the desires of the flesh and of the mind" (vs. 3), i.e., the desires *produced by* the flesh and the mind. The two sources of evil desire are thus the unregenerate nature ("flesh")[2] and the perverted thoughts and imaginations of the unrenewed mind (cf. Rom. 8:7).

3. *Objects of Divine Wrath* (vs. 3b). Both Jews and Gentiles, Paul affirms, are "by nature children of wrath" (ASV). The expression "children of wrath" describes people as not only worthy of the divine wrath but as actually subject to it. The NEB translates, "We . . . lay under the dreadful judgement of God." The expression is a Hebraism, and is similar in usage to "children of disobedience" in verse 2.

Many moderns think of God as an easygoing, good-natured, grandfatherly Being. To them the idea of a God of wrath is unthinkable. But both the Old and the New Testaments have much to say about the wrath of God. His wrath is a permanent and consistent element in His nature and is best seen as the reverse side of His holy love. God's wrath represents the divine hostility to all that is evil. It is a personal quality without which God could not be fully righteous. Nor is His wrath inconsistent with His love, for without righteous wrath love easily degenerates into mere sentimentality.

Paul declares that men are children of wrath "by nature." There are interpreters who see these words as simply drawing a marked contrast between what men are in grace and what they are "naturally," apart from grace (cf. NEB, "in our natural condition"; Robinson, "in ourselves," p. 156). Other interpreters contend that the phrase "by nature" describes that which is innate. According to this view, there is a principle of sin in man by nature, and man sins because of that innate principle. "We are sinners *in grain*; every mother's son learns to be naughty without book" (Simpson, p. 49). Unregenerate men are therefore objects of divine wrath, not merely because of what they have done but also because of what they are. Cf. TCNT, "Our very nature exposed us to the Divine Wrath."

[2]Some interpreters give to the word "flesh" in this phrase a meaning different from that which it has in the immediately preceding phrase. The TEV, for example, interprets "lusts of our flesh" (in the first phrase) to mean "natural desires." In the second phrase it takes "of the flesh and of the mind" to mean "our own bodies and minds" (cf. RSV).

II. The Christian Position (2:4-6)

Paul has shown that sin and death and wrath are the common experiences of the unregenerate, whether they are Jews (like himself) or Gentiles (like his readers). Against that dark background he will now show the wealth of divine grace and love and what these have done for persons who have put their trust in Christ. In a sense, then, the delineation of verses 1-3 is only preparatory to what is said in verses 4-6. Man's sin and God's wrath serve as the dark background against which the riches of God's mercy and the greatness of His love and grace shine forth the more brilliantly.

The present passage strikingly contrasts the past and present conditions of believers. Once they were objects of God's wrath; now they are recipients of His mercy (vs. 4). Once they were held in the grip of spiritual death; now they have been raised to new life (vss. 5,6). Once they were in bondage to sin; now they are saved by grace (vs. 5). Once they walked among the disobedient; now they enjoy fellowship with God's Son (vss. 5,6).

1. *Recipients of Divine Mercy* (vs. 4). Two things are emphasized in verse 4. First, God alone is the author of the change believers experience upon entering the Christian life. Second, and more specifically, this change is grounded in the boundless mercy and great love of God. "Mercy" (Greek, *eleos*) speaks of God's compassion and pity for helpless sinners; "love" (Greek, *agape*) is that divine disposition that sees something infinitely precious in people in spite of their sin. Both of these things move God to deliver man from his sinful predicament.

The conjunction of God's wrath (vs. 3) and his love and mercy (vs. 4) is not without significance. The apostle has just spoken of Jew and Gentile as alike "children of wrath." Here he affirms God's "great love" for those same persons, even when dead in sin: "It seems necessary to place the two momentous facts in association, in order to gain a proper conception of either. Upon the one hand, the 'wrath' . . . is not of that implacable kind which the word, as so often in popular speech, might denote; while, upon the other, the 'love' is by no means the love of mere indulgence. . . . His love does not blind him to the sin; neither does the sin so alienate the love as that no further thought of kindness and no provision of grace can be hoped for" (Smith, p. 36).

2. *Resurrected to New Life* (vss. 5,6). In verses 5,6 Paul recounts three experiences of believers that are traceable to divine mercy and love. These are: a spiritual quickening, a spiritual resurrection, and a spiritual exaltation. They are the counterparts of the literal quickening, resurrection, and exaltation of Christ (cf. 1:20-23).

Verse 5 is best translated, "Even when we were dead through our trespasses, God made us alive together with Christ" (ASV). With these words Paul resumes the thought of verse 1. The central words are, "hath quickened us together with Christ." To quicken means to make alive, to impart life, the idea being practically equivalent to regeneration.

This quickening took place "even when we were dead through our trespasses." This remarkable statement emphasizes both the greatness of God's power and the richness of His mercy. Notwithstanding our miserable condition, even while we were held in the grip of spiritual death, God intervened on our behalf and actually communicated spiritual life to us. "Together with Christ" does not mean that He and we were quickened in the same way. The words express the ideas of union and fellowship. The new life that is ours is not only made possible by Christ; it is shared with Him.

To emphasize that the believer's redemption in Christ is given freely, Paul inserts by way of a parenthesis: "By grace ye are saved" (vs. 5b). "By grace" suggests that men are undeserving sinners with absolutely no claim on the mercy of God. "Ye are saved" translates a tense that views salvation as an act completed in the past but continuous and permanent in its results. To put it otherwise, the stress is not on the act of being saved, but on the fact of having been saved. The whole clause means that our having been brought into a state or condition of salvation was due wholly to the pure, free favor of God. It comes in as a sort of exclamation and shows how anxious Paul was to see that the gratuitous nature of salvation should never be forgotten. The thought is repeated and expanded in verse 8.

Verse 6 mentions two further results of the mercy and love of God in the lives of believers. Not only has He quickened us, but He has also "raised us up" and "made us sit together in heavenly places." The first phrase refers to the spiritual resurrection Christians experience in conversion. The latter words are also to be interpreted spiritually. Both expressions (raised us up," "made us sit together") amplify and expand the truth of the verb "quickened." That is to say, the quickening includes the being raised and the being seated with Christ; it is these experiences that bring the new life out into manifestation. As a parallel, one might note that Christ was quickened before He came out of Joseph's tomb, but His leaving the tomb was an open manifestation of His new resurrection life.

Each of these verbs ("quickened," "raised," and "made . . . sit") expresses what God has already done for His people. We accept the truth that the quickening and the resurrection are spiritual realities from the very moment of conversion. But it staggers the imagination to be told that the enthronement with Christ is already an accomplished fact. Paul is presenting the matter from God's point of view, and in the mind of God our position in Christ is fixed and certain.

On "heavenly places" (vs. 6) see the discussion of 1:3. Blaikie understands the phrase to denote "places where the privileges of heaven are dispensed, where the air of heaven is breathed, where the fellowship and enjoyment of heaven are known, where an elevation of spirit is experienced as if heaven were begun" (pp. 62,63).

The key to the blessed experience of the resurrected, enthroned life is really the phrase "in Christ Jesus" (vs. 6), for it is in virtue of our union with Christ that we share His life and exaltation. In the words of H. C. G. Moule: "We are *beside* Him there upon His seat of victory and dominion, because we are embodied *in* Him, by the Spirit's power and in the bond of faith" (*Ephesian Studies*, p. 76).

3. *Fellowship With the Living Christ* (vss. 5,6). Observe the use of the word "together" in verses 5,6. There may be some slight allusion to the experiences believers share with one another, but the word mainly speaks of an association or fellowship that believers have with Christ. The idea is in bold contrast to the description of their former life as lived among, and shared with, "the children of disobedience" (vss. 2,3).

Each of the three principal verbs in the Greek is a compound form suggesting association — "made-alive-together-with," "raised-up-together-with," and "made-to-sit-together-with." These verbs should be compared with the parallel phrases concerning Christ, as used in 1:20, where we are told that God "raised" Christ and "set" Him at His right hand. The believer, by his union with Christ, shares in what God has done for Christ. The truth is almost too glorious to comprehend. No wonder Paul recorded the prayer of 1:17,18.

III. THE DIVINE PURPOSE (2:7-10)

Why has God done all of this for believers? A part of the answer has already been given. God has acted on account of his "great love where with he loved us" (vs. 4). Those words, however, speak specifically of God's *motive* in quickening and raising believers. The full statement of *purpose* must be found in verses 7-10. Two ideas may be discerned. The first is elaborated in verses 7-9. It speaks of God's intention to make believers an eternal display of His grace. The second idea (vs. 10) declares that His purpose was to make possible a life of good works on the part of believers. These two ideas are not entirely separate and distinct. The manifestation of God's grace and the holiness of His people are both intended to redound to God's glory.

1. *To Exhibit the Wealth of Divine Grace* (vss. 7-9). Believers are

trophies of God's grace, and it is His design that in them the surpassing wealth of that grace may be forever exhibited. The words "he might shew" (vs. 7) translate a Greek word that might be used of a demonstration or an exhibition. (Cf. NEB, "that he might display.") That which God intends to demonstrate is the "exceeding riches of his grace" (vs. 7). (Paul has previously spoken of the wealth of God's grace [1:7], the wealth of the glory of God's inheritance [1:18], and the wealth of mercy [2:4]. Here the addition of the word "exceeding" points to the superlative greatness of divine grace.) This marvelous demonstration of grace is seen in the "kindness" that God has bestowed on believers "through [in] Christ Jesus" (vs. 7). He lavishes His kindness on us by quickening, raising, and enthroning us with Christ. We, then, become monuments of His grace, or channels through whom the truth of that grace is made known to all creation. (Note the piling up of words showing God's benevolent attitude toward men — mercy, love, grace, kindness.)

Some interpreters have applied the phrase "in the ages to come" to the generations from the time of Paul to the second coming of Christ. It is more likely, however, that the "ages to come" are those that follow the second coming of Christ. Paul had in mind the grand display of God's wondrous grace in eternity. The plural, suggesting a succession of ages, heightens the thought of endlessness.

Verses 8,9, perhaps the most familiar verses in Ephesians, are intended to confirm and amplify the statement of verse 7. They tell how the salvation of men can be the exhibition of grace that Paul has declared it to be. (Observe the word "for" that begins verse 8.) It is because salvation from start to finish is God's work.

The thought clusters around three great gospel words: *saved*, *grace*, and *faith*. They are so frequently used that they may have become somewhat threadbare, but this is all the more reason for making sure that we understand them. The first word, when used in a theological sense, as here, speaks of a rescue and suggests the imminent peril from which we have been delivered in Christ. "Ye are saved" is the translation of a Greek perfect tense. It points to a decisive experience in the past (an act completed), but it also emphasizes a present and continuing condition growing out of that past act. The meaning is: You were saved (at some point in the past) and are now in a state or condition of salvation. (Cf. the discussion of vs. 5.)

From God's point of view, salvation is complete, though on our side it may be seen as in progress. (Cf. 1 Cor. 1:18, where a present progressive tense is used: "are being saved," ASV, margin.) The experience has been likened to that of a man in a shipwreck. From the moment he is taken out of the icy water into the lifeboat, he is a saved man. He may scarcely feel his safety or be relieved from his fears; indeed, there may pass many long hours before his feet touch the dry land and his rescue is complete. Nonetheless, from the moment he is in the boat he is safe.

The phrase "by grace," which has the place of emphasis in verse 8, expresses the means by which men are saved — not by weeping, not by their own willing, not through their own works or efforts, but by grace. But what is grace? The word is used more than one hundred fifty times in the New Testament (almost a hundred times by Paul alone) and with a variety of meanings. But its basic meaning is that of favor shown to the utterly undeserving. The TCNT translates it "loving-kindness"; Goodspeed, "mercy"; Williams, "unmerited favor." The idea, then, is that salvation is a bounty from God, not a reward for merit.

Salvation is by grace, but it is also "through faith." This statement does not teach that faith is a meritorious ground or procuring cause of salvation. It asserts rather that faith is the appropriating means; it is the hand that receives the gift. Compare Knox's rendering: "Yes, it was grace that saved you, with faith for its instrument." "Faith," says Calvin, "brings a man empty to God, that he may be filled with the blessings of Christ" (p. 227). The word itself means trust or reliance upon. The NEB translates, "For it is by grace you are saved, through trusting him."

To strengthen yet more the thought that salvation is wholly a work of God, the apostle adds, "and that not of yourselves: it is the gift of God: not of works, lest any man should boast" (vss. 8,9). Calvin sums up Paul's meaning as follows:

> In these three phrases, — not of yourselves, — it is the gift of God, — not of works, — he [Paul] embraces the substance of his long argument in the Epistles to the Romans and to the Galatians, that righteousness comes to us from the mercy of God alone, — is offered to us in Christ by the gospel, — and is received by faith alone, without the merit of works (p. 228).

The only word calling for further explanation is the pronoun *that*. In the English translation it seems to have its antecedent in the word *faith*. The thought would then be that even faith is a gift of God. Theologically this interpretation is quite correct (cf. Phil. 1:29). But from the grammatical point of view, "that" here seems to refer to the whole process of salvation (i.e., the entire thought of vs. 8), which, of course, includes faith. Since salvation is so completely God's work and since human achievement is so conclusively ruled out, it is little wonder that there is no room for any man to boast. All praise must be given to God and his grace.

> Come, Thou Fount of ev'ry blessing,
> Tune my heart to sing Thy grace;

Streams of mercy, never ceasing,
    Call for songs of loudest praise:
Teach me some melodious sonnet,
    Sung by flaming tongues above;
Praise the mount — I'm fixed upon it —
    Mount of Thy redeeming love.

O to grace how great a debtor
    Daily I'm constrained to be!
Let Thy goodness, like a fetter,
    Bind my wond'ring heart to Thee:
Prone to wander, Lord, I feel it,
    Prone to leave the God I love;
Here's my heart, O take and seal it,
    Seal it for thy courts above.

— Robert Robinson

2. *To Make Possible a Life of Good Works* (vs. 10). Verse 10 is designed to enforce and give a reason for the great truth of verses 8,9. Salvation cannot be of works "for" (because, since) believers are themselves the handiwork of God. The Greek word for "workmanship," the essential meaning of which is "a thing made," was used for any finished product, especially for a work of art, such as a painting, a sculptured stone, or a piece of literature. It is used elsewhere in the New Testament only in Romans 1:20, where it refers to the material creation and is translated "the things that are made." All about us we see the works of God's hands. "The heavens declare the glory of God; and the firmament sheweth his handiwork" (Psalm 19:1). But God's greatest work, his *masterpiece*, is a new creature in Christ Jesus.

In the phrase "created in Christ Jesus," the use of the word "created" shows how radical and transforming the experience of salvation is. The change it effects is so great that Paul can speak of the saved man as a new creation. "In Christ Jesus" means "in union with Christ Jesus."

The stress of this entire verse is on the phrase "unto [for] good works." These words express the end that was in view when we were recreated in Christ. One must distinguish clearly between good works as the ground of salvation and good works as the proof and fruit of salvation. We are not saved *by* good works, but most assuredly we are saved *for* them. As Paul expresses it in another place, Christ gave Himself for us "that he might redeem us from all iniquity, and purify unto himself a people for his own possession, zealous of good works" (Titus 2:14, ASV). Those therefore who have believed in God should be "careful to maintain good works" (Titus 3:8).

These good works God "prepared that we should walk in them" (ASV). They are not mere incidental accompaniments of the Christian life; they are a part of God's eternal plan for His people. We are created for them; they await our doing.

SUMMARY

These verses constitute one of the great passages of the Bible and contain a veritable mine of spiritual truth. They teach, for example, that all people are by nature in bondage to sin; that salvation must be traced to God's grace and mercy, not to any supposed merit on our part; that faith in Christ is the means of appropriating God's offer of grace; that a life of obedience is the end result of salvation. The last three verses in particular express in clear and concentrated form the very essense of the gospel.

The heart of the entire paragraph centers in what God has done for us in Christ. Something of the richness of the experience is suggested by the three principal figures used to describe it: life, salvation, and re-creation. Reflection on these things will not only expand our understanding of the Christian experience but will also deepen and enrich our relationship with God.

The tone of these verses, however, is not solely theological. They remind us that what we have experienced in Christ has far-reaching, practical implications for our lives. We are God's workmanship, "created" in Christ Jesus unto [with a view to the performance of] good works." The following are only a few of the ways in which we should give proof of the presence of divine grace in our lives.

1. *The expression of gratitude.* Grace makes us debtors to God. Therefore, by our speech and by our life we should show forth our praise and thanks to Him.

2. *The cultivation of character.* A religion that does not express itself in character is worthless. Salvation is not a bare deliverance from the penalty of sin. It is the beginning of a new life that is intended to grow more and more Christlike. Only as this happens can we be the instruments through whom God makes His grace known to the world.

3. *The performance of good works.* We have often been so afraid someone would accuse us of teaching salvation by works that we have not done full justice to the biblical emphasis on works as the fruit and proof of salvation.

Jesus went about doing good. We should do the same. We should minister to the needs of the poor in our communities, share our substance with the starving millions around our world, help the homeless, befriend the friendless, care for the sick and suffering. In short, the compassion we profess must be translated into positive deeds of kindness.

FOR FURTHER STUDY

1. Consider how the statements of Ephesians 2:1-3 apply to all unbelievers.

2. Using a concordance, study the words *grace, faith, salvation, works*, etc.

3. Read "Life From the Dead" in Spurgeon's *Treasury of the Bible: New Testament*.

4. Maclaren's *Expositions of Holy Scripture* contains four sermons on Ephesians 2:1-10.

CHAPTER 6

The Formation of God's New People: By the Reconciliation of Jew and Gentile in Christ

(Ephesians 2:11-22)

The first half of chapter 2 has told of the spiritual death in which both Jew and Gentile were once held and of the quickening that they experienced as individuals. The last half emphasizes the corporate experience of believers and tells how, through the redemption in Christ, Jew and Gentile have been made into "one new man."

The relationship of these two races in the first Christian century may seem to be of little concern to people of the twentieth century, but several considerations make it significant. For one thing, it was a burning issue in the apostle's time. F. F. Bruce observes that "no iron curtain, colour bar, class distinction or national frontier of today is more absolute than the cleavage between Jew and Gentile was in antiquity." He goes on to declare that the transformation that enabled Jew and Gentile to become truly one in Christ was the "greatest triumph of the gospel in the apostolic age" (p. 54).

What is stated in this passage in terms of the reconciliation of Jew and Gentile involves a very precious principle that is of significance for every age. That principle is movingly stated by John Oxenham in the words that we often sing:

> In Christ there is no East or West,
> In Him no South or North.

But alas! the words of James Denney, written more than half a century ago, are uncomfortably close to being a picture of our times:

> Of all Christian truths which are confessed in words, this is that which is most outrageously denied in deed. There is not a Christian church nor a Christian nation in the world which believes heartily in the Atonement as the extinction of privilege, and the levelling up of all men to the same possibility of life in Christ, to the same calling to be saints. The spirit of privilege, in spite of the Cross, is obstinately rooted everywhere even among Christian men (p. 201).

Ephesians 2:11-22 shows how, even in Paul's day, God's great purpose of unity had already begun to be realized in Christ (cf. 1:10). The wall of partition that had kept the Gentile at a distance had been broken down; in Christ redeemed Jews and redeemed Gentiles, representing the two hostile sections of humanity, had been reconciled to one another; and through Him both walked hand in hand into the presence of God.

The paragraph (vss. 11-22) falls quite naturally into two divisions, marked off by the words "in time past" (vs. 11) and "but now" (vs. 13). The former phrase alludes to the condition of the Gentiles before conversion, the latter refers to their position in Christ.

I. THE FORMER CONDITION OF THE GENTILES (2:11,12)

The first word of verse 11, "wherefore," arrests attention and relates that which follows to the topic of discussion in 2:1-10. In view of their gracious experience of spiritual transformation, the apostle calls on his Gentile readers to keep on remembering what they once were apart from God's grace. It is most appropriate for all the children of grace to summon themselves to such recollections. To do so is to deepen our appreciation of the mercy and grace of God and make us more thankful, more humble.

The pre-Christian condition of the Gentiles is summed up in two statements: They were objects of Jewish contempt (vs. 11), and they were spiritually bankrupt (vs. 12).

1. *Objects of Jewish Contempt* (vs. 11). So intense was the Jewish contempt for the Gentile that it was not even lawful for a Jew to assist a Gentile woman in her hour of childbirth. The marriage of a Jew to a Gentile was looked upon as the equivalent of death, and the death rites of the Jewish boy or girl entering such a union were immediately carried out. Even to enter a Gentile house made a Jew ceremonially unclean.

In verse 11 Paul reminds his readers of this abhorrence the Jews had for them. They were "Gentiles in the flesh" and were contemptuously referred to as "the Uncircumcision." "Gentiles" means what we mean today by the terms "pagan" or "heathen." To be Gentiles "in the flesh" means to be Gentiles (pagans) "by birth" (TEV) or "outwardly" (NEB). Weymouth translates the entire phrase "Gentiles as to your bodily condition." The words are an obvious allusion to the Gentiles' lack of participation in the Mosaic rite of circumcision. Their very bodies proclaimed their pagan character, the outward mark of uncircumcision being a symbol of their irreligion and debasement.

Paul is careful to make it clear, however, that the Jew who would speak so contemptuously of the Gentile was not all that he should have been. The Jews proudly called themselves "the Circumcision," but Paul knew that for them this symbol of their separation was all too often a mere outward rite void of any true spiritual reality. Theirs was a circumcision "in the flesh made by hands." The NEB says they were " 'the circumcised' (but only with reference to an outward rite)" (vs. 11b). (Cf. Rom. 2:28,29; Phil. 3:3; Col. 2:11.)

2. *Spiritually Bankrupt* (vs. 12). "That at that time" (vs. 12) resumes the thought begun with "remember" in verse 11. The readers are now reminded that there was true spiritual deprivation involved in their being Gentiles. Paul sums it up in five descriptive phrases, each of which is negative.

First, they were "without Christ." The Greek expression might better be translated "apart from the Christ" (cf. TEV), the idea being that in their former condition they had no connection with the Messiah; they were completely lacking in any true relation to Him. For centuries the Jews had cherished the hope of the Messiah. Their understanding of His mission might sometimes have been very inadequate, but even in the darkest hours of their history they never doubted that He would come. From this expectation they drew strength and courage. But the Gentiles neither expected nor knew of the Messiah.

Beare speaks of "without Christ" as the negative counterpart of "in Christ." The doxology of 1:3-14 "recounts the blessings which come to men *in Christ*; here the writer gives a summary of the disabilities of man *without Christ*." He sees the four phrases that follow as "an outline in detail of what this separation involved" (p. 651).

Second, they were "aliens from the commonwealth of Israel." The word "aliens" expresses the general idea of separation and estrangement. The "commonwealth of Israel" speaks of the Israelitish nation as the realm or society in which the sovereignty of God took earthly shape and found expression. It was the sphere within which God made Himself known to men and entered into relation with them. Gentiles, so long as they were "without Christ," had no part in that order. They were not at home with the people of God. They were outside the circle of those who worshiped Him.

Third, the Gentiles were "strangers from the covenants of promise." The reference is to the covenants (agreements) pertaining to the promise of the Messiah. The plural is used to indicate that the one covenant, originally made with Abraham, was often renewed with, and reaffirmed for, his descendants (cf. Rom. 9:4). The word for "strangers" carries the idea of being foreign to a thing, having no share in it.

Fourth, since they were strangers from the covenants of promise, the Gentiles had "no hope." Paul does not mean that they had no aspirations and desires, for many Gentiles desired better things. There was a deep hunger on the part of many for spiritual deliverance. But mere desire is not hope. Hope is a blending of desire with expectation, and this the Gentile world did not have. The literature of the age and inscriptions on tombstones provide unimpeachable evidence that the Gentile world bade an eternal farewell to their loved ones when they laid their bodies in the grave. They had no hope that death should ever be "destroyed" or "swallowed up in victory" (1 Cor. 15:26,54). "Their future," writes Eadie, "was a night without a star" (p. 167).

The melancholy that had long enshrouded the ancient pagan world had by New Testament times deepened into unrelieved gloom. Life was so full of trouble, so haunted by black destiny, so brief and uncertain that many people felt that the best thing of all was not to be born, and the next best thing was to die. The despair of the ancient Gentile world is aptly described in Matthew Arnold's lines:

> On that hard Pagan world disgust
> And secret loathing fell;
> Deep weariness and sated lust
> Made human life a hell.

Finally, the Gentiles were "without God in the world." To have no hope for the future is bad enough; to have no God in the present makes the situation unspeakably tragic. The Greek word is *atheoi*. It does not mean, however, that the Gentiles were atheists, for they had "gods many and lords many." The apostle means that they did not have the knowledge of, nor any saving relationship to, the one true God (1 Cor. 8:4-6). The "world" may be mentioned in contrast with "commonwealth." If so, there is stress on the world as evil, as dark and hostile and under Satan's dominion. In such a world of sin and death, of shame and sorrow and suffering, Gentiles had no God to guide, to befriend, to bless, and to save them.

II. THE NEW RELATIONSHIP OF THE GENTILES (2:13-22)

With verse 13 Paul turns from the past to the present. "But now" contrasts with "at that time" (vs. 12). "In Christ Jesus," which suggests being in union with Him (cf. NEB), is set over against the words "without [apart from] Christ" (vs. 12). The principal teachings of the passage may be summed up in three statements: (1) In Christ Jesus Gentile and Jew are reconciled to one another (vss. 13-15). (2) In Christ Jesus Gentile and Jew are at peace with God (vss. 16-18). (3) In Christ Jesus Gentile and Jew share alike in the privileges and blessings of the gospel (vss. 19-22).

1. *Gentile and Jew Reconciled to One Another* (vss. 13-16). Once, apart from the Christ, the Gentiles "were far off" (vs. 13). Now, by virtue of being "in Christ Jesus," these same people "are made nigh" (vs. 13). To be "far off" is simply a way of restating in a summary fashion all that

Paul had said of the Gentiles in verses 11-21. Israel, by virtue of their covenant relationship to God, enjoyed nearness to him; the Gentiles lived at a distance, being alienated from God and separated from His people.

The being "made nigh" appears on the surface to relate exclusively to the Gentiles' being brought near to God. This idea undoubtedly is the primary meaning, for both Jew and Gentile must draw near to God before they can draw near to one another. However, both nearness to God and incorporation among His people are included in the words. In verses 14, 15 the thought definitely centers in the relationship of Jew and Gentile to one another.

The means by which this new relationship is effected is stated in verse 13b: "Ye . . . were made nigh by the blood of Christ." "Blood" points up the sacrificial character of Christ's death (cf. discussion of 1:7). The TCNT expands the term to mean "shedding of blood."

Verses 14-16 explain more fully the various aspects of this reconciliation. The essence of it is that by the death of Christ the exclusiveness of the theocracy was abolished; Jew and Gentile, by the abrogation of the Mosaic law, are placed on the same level; and both, in the blood of Christ, are reconciled to God. The passage bristles with exegetical difficulties, but limited space will not permit discussion of all of them. Only those most essential to a correct interpretation can be treated.

The apostle begins by declaring that "he [Christ] is our peace" (vs. 14a). That is to say, Christ not only *makes* peace by His death but He *is* in Himself the very substance and living source of it. The pronoun ("he") is emphatic. In NEB this is translated, "For he is himself our peace."

Next, Paul asserts that Christ in his death "made both" Jew and Gentile "one" and broke down "the middle wall of partition" between them (vs. 14). "Both" refers to the two ethnic groups — Jews and Gentiles. "One" in Greek is a neuter word here, conveying the thought that Christ in His death made these two antagonistic parties a unity. They are "not changed in race, nor amalgamated in blood, but they are 'one' in point of privilege and position toward God" (Eadie, p. 171).

The "middle wall of partition" (RSV, "dividing wall") is a figurative description of the barrier that existed between Jew and Gentile. Likely there is an allusion to the wall in the Jerusalem temple that separated the court of the Gentiles from the sanctuary proper. At various places along this wall there were signs in Hebrew and Greek forbidding Gentiles to pass beyond it on pain of death. That barrier with its inscribed stones was still standing when Paul wrote Ephesians, and he used it as a tangible symbol of the enmity separating Jew and Gentile.

In the KJV the word *enmity* (vs. 15) is taken with the words that follow it. That is to say, the "enmity" is defined as "the law of commandments." In the Greek text, however, the word for "enmity" may be understood as being in apposition with the expression "the middle wall." Thus, the wall is the hostility existing between Jew and Gentile. Note the following translations: NEB, "the enmity which stood like a dividing wall between them; RSV, "the dividing wall of hostility."

The dividing wall of hostility between the two races was removed when Christ "in his flesh" (i.e., His incarnate state, and especially the death He endured in that state) abolished the "law of commandments" (vs. 15, RSV). Thus, the law is seen as in some sense a hindrance to unity between Jew and Gentile. The legal system embodied in the law of Moses was of divine origin and was intended to protect Israel from the paganism of surrounding nations. Yet this system, misinterpreted and abused, in time became a source of Jewish pride and exclusiveness in relation to the Gentiles.

"Having abolished" translates a participle that modifies "hath broken down." It tells the means by which the middle wall was destroyed. The RSV has "[He] has broken down the dividing wall of hostility, by abolishing in his flesh. . . ." The word itself means to make ineffective or to nullify, the thought here being that Christ has abrogated the law.

The question naturally arises: In what sense has the law been abrogated? Some interpreters see in the statement a reference to the setting aside of the ceremonial law because of the fulfillment in Christ of all that it typified. Others understand the reference to be to the whole Moasic law. Paul's definition appears to lend support to the latter view. He calls it "the law of commandments contained in [expressed by] ordinances [decrees]" (vs. 15). The thought is of an elaborate system or code ("law") comprised of minute regulations and prescriptions ("commandments") and expressed by, or couched in, revealed edicts ("decrees"). Such a legal system is viewed as a barrier between the two racial groups, and Christ has rendered it inoperative by His death.

A similar idea is expressed in Colossians 2:14, where Paul declares that Christ has blotted out "the handwriting [bond] of indebtedness . . . that was against us, . . . nailing it to his cross." In the Colossians passage the law is viewed as an instrument of condemnation or as a legal note of indebtedness for which we were liable but the demands of which we were unable to satisfy. Christ by His death paid our debt, canceled the bond, and took it forever out of the way. The imagery of the Colossians passage is different from that of its Ephesians parallel, and the application of its truth is somewhat different; but the main burden of the two passages is essentially the same.

Whether the law be viewed as a wall dividing race from race or as an instrument of condemnation, Christ has nullified it, taken it out of the way. By the removal of the Mosaic system the hostility between Jew and Gentile was destroyed, and the dividing wall that kept them apart was laid low.

The divine purpose in abrogating the law is stated in verses 15b, 16. *First*, it was that Christ might "make in himself of twain [Jew and Gentile] one new man" (vs. 15b). Weymouth translates, "His design was to unite the two sections of humanity in Himself so as to form one new man"; TEV, "to create out of the two races a single new people." This statement is an advance on verse 14. It is not simply that the two races are made into one man, but into one *new* man. Moreover, the thought is not merely that the two races are brought together, with the Jew remaining a Jew and the Gentile continuing as a Gentile. Nor is it that the Gentile becomes a Jew, nor that the Jew becomes a Gentile. The idea is of the creation out of the two of something entirely new — a new humanity, a new people of God.

This "new man" is created in Christ ("himself"). He lays one hand on the Jew, the other on the Gentile, and brings the two together in Himself. So long as Jew and Gentile are unbelievers, they continue to be at enmity with one another. It is only as each is united to Christ that they come to be at harmony, one with the other.

The *second* purpose in the annulment of the law is expressed in verse 16: "that he might reconcile both Jew and Gentile together unto God in one body." Here the emphasis shifts from the relationship between Jew and Gentile to the relationship of both to God. Though brought in second in the passage, this concept is undoubtedly first in importance. It is developed more fully in verses 17, 18.

2. *Gentile and Jew at Peace With God* (vss. 16-18). Christ not only unites Jew and Gentile into one new man; He also reconciles both to God. The two acts, though stated separately, are actually simultaneous. The union of the two hostile races is intimately bound up with, and indeed is based on, the larger concept of reconciliation to God; for the death of enmity among men is conditioned on the death of their enmity against God. The "one body" is not Christ's physical body but rather His mystical or spiritual body, of which believing Jews and believing Gentiles are both members. Christ desired to "bring the two long-sundered and antagonistic parties as one whole, one great body, into right relation to God by His cross" (Salmond, p. 297).

This is one of the four New Testament passages that treat the work of Christ under the figure of reconciliation. (The others are Rom. 5:10f.; 2 Cor. 5:18ff.; Col. 1:19ff.) The word "reconcile" suggests a change of relations between God and man and implies a previous state of estrangement and enmity. Note carefully that it is not God who is reconciled to man, but man who is reconciled to God. The New Testament always presents this point of view, for it is man's sin that has caused the enmity.

The meaning is not, however, that Christ's reconciling activities are concerned only with man. Reconciliation is not purely a subjective process. It was in some sense effected outside of man before anything happened within him. This idea is implied in Paul's words in Romans 5:11, "through whom we have now received the reconciliation" (ASV). A reconciliation that can be received must in some sense be an accomplished fact before one receives it. In other words, reconciliation is both Godward and manward. The death of Jesus removes the offending sin from man's heart and turns away the divine wrath. Man receives, or accepts, what God has wrought.

Christ by His death secured peace. He also preached the glad tidings of it "to you [Gentiles] which were afar off, and to them that were nigh [the Jews]" (vs. 17; cf. Isa. 52:7; 57:19). The peace mentioned is, of course, that which has been under discussion throughout this passage — peace between Jew and Gentile and peace between both and God. The question that arises from this statement is *when* and *how* this preaching was done. That the statement here cannot refer to Christ's personal ministry on earth is clear from two considerations. First, the preaching of peace to the Gentiles did not characterize His ministry on earth. Second, the context of verse 17 suggests that the preaching followed the accomplishment of reconciliation on the cross. We conclude, then, that the coming referred to (vs. 17) was Christ's coming in the Spirit and the preaching was that done by Christ through His apostles and other believers.

Verse 18 affords proof that peace has been secured and announced for both Jews and Gentiles: "For through him we both [Jews and Gentiles] have access by one Spirit unto the Father." Every word is important. "For" shows the connection of the sentence with what has gone before. "Access," a word used by the ancients of the introduction of someone to a royal court, speaks here both of unhindered approach to God and of actual introduction into the divine presence (cf. Rom. 5:2). In the Old Testament economy only the high priest could enter into the holy of holies, and that only once each year. But in Christ all believers have continual access. "Both" emphasizes that this privilege is shared by Jew and Gentile alike. The prepositions in the sentence are very meaningful and deserving of careful consideration. Our access is "through" Christ, "by" (better, "in") the Spirit, and "to" the Father. The doctrine of the Trinity, though not explicitly taught here, is obviously implied.

3. *Gentile and Jew Sharing the Privileges and Blessings of the Gospel* (vss. 19-22). Verses 19-22 draw a number of inferences from the teaching set forth in verses 13-18. These all have to do with the new fellowship into which believing Jews and believing Gentiles have been brought. The emphasis, however, is on the elevation of the Gentile to a position of equal privilege and benefit. Three figures are used to express this: a nation, a family, and a building.

With regard to the first of these figures, Paul assures his Gentile readers that they are "no more strangers and foreigners, but fellow citizens with the saints" (vs. 19). They have been spiritually enfranchised. "Strangers and foreigners" was a comprehensive expression including all who for various reasons did not enjoy the full rights of citizenship in a city or nation. Once this was the condition of the Gentiles in regard to the theocracy of Israel (cf. 2:11,12), but no longer is it so. "Saints" is a name for the people of God, the whole community of believers (see discussion of 1:1). In Christ national restrictions have been removed, and all Gentile believers are a part of the true "Israel of God" (Gal. 6:16). They share alike, with all who belong to it, the privileges and benefits of the new spiritual commonwealth.

The political figure gives way (vs. 19) to a domestic one. Paul's readers are not only "fellow-citizens with the saints," they are also members "of the household [family] of God." This statement suggests that the fellowship of believers is of the closest, warmest kind. But beyond this idea, it speaks of the intimate relationship that all Christians sustain to God. They are His family and may address Him as Father.

Verse 20 introduces the figure of a building. Believing Gentiles, along with believing Jews, are being built into a great spiritual structure "upon the foundation of the apostles and prophets, Jesus Christ himself being the chief cornerstone."

How are we to understand "the foundation of the apostles and prophets"? Are the apostles and prophets themselves the foundation? Or does the statement mean that the foundation is laid by them? Paul in another place says, "Other foundation can no man lay than that is laid, which is Jesus Christ" (1 Cor. 3:11). However, since the relation of Christ to the building is in this passage expressed by another figure ("chief cornerstone"), it is probably better to think of the foundation as *consisting* of the apostles and prophets. (The context suggests that these are New Testament prophets, of whom more will be said later [cf. 3:5; 4:11].) Christ, then, is chief cornerstone; apostles and prophets are the foundation; other believers are the superstructure.

Beare says the cornerstone is "the stone placed at the summit of the edifice as its crown and completion" (p. 661). Moule, on the other hand, takes the cornerstone to be the great stone put in the angle of the substructure where the walls met. It was the stone on which the stability of the whole building depended. Christ as chief cornerstone is thus the one who supports and holds together both the foundation and the walls. It is He who gives to this wondrous spiritual edifice its unity and its strength. Indeed, everything ultimately depends on Him.

Paul adds that in union with Christ ("in whom") "all the building" by being "fitly framed together" is growing [like a living organism] into a "holy temple [sanctuary] in the Lord" (vs. 21). He reminds his readers of the part they have in this glorious structure. They (and believers of every age) who once were without hope and without God in the world are now being "builded together." The process is going on "through [by] the Spirit," to produce "a habitation of God" (vs. 22). The entire building process has as its goal the perfecting of a great spiritual dwelling place (spoken of in vs. 21 as a "temple," and in vs. 22 as a "habitation") for God.

Differences of opinion about verses 21,22 center largely in the phrase "all the building" (vs. 21). The renderings of KJV, RSV, NEB, and others suggest the picture of one great spiritual building that grows (both in compactness and in size) as each new believer is added to the structure (cf. 1 Peter 2:5). The imagery in ASV is that of a number of smaller buildings being joined together so as to form one whole structure. Some interpreters see an allusion to the many buildings and courts that made up the Jerusalem temple. They understand Paul's words as referring to the many local congregations ("each several building") increasing in number and completeness so as to form together one great holy temple in the Lord (see Carver).

There is a remarkable contrast between the way chapter 2 begins — death in trespasses and sins — and the way it closes — believers a holy temple indwelt by God.

In looking back over Ephesians 2:11-21, we should take note of the following thoughts that the passage suggests: First, *the persistence of walls that divide men*. The ancient world was a world of dividing walls. Everywhere there were barriers of custom, suspicion, and hostility. The Jew held the Gentile in complete contempt. The Roman was suspicious of the Jew and bitterly resented his presence. Greeks looked down on all non-Greeks and lumped them together under the unflattering term "barbarian." In addition to this, everywhere there was the wall of sin that man had erected between himself and God. After twenty centuries there are still dividing walls in our world. Most of us are painfully aware of the barriers that zigzag and crisscross through modern society. Class is set against class, nation against nation, and race against race.

Second, *the power of Christ's cross*. The barriers that divide men do not have to exist. The unity Christ effected between Jew and Gentile in the first century is a striking witness to the power of His gospel to deal effectively with all of the discord and hostility of every century. However, it is only as people submit to the claims of Christ and live by the power of His cross that the barriers that divide them will crumble to the earth.

Third, *the fellowship of God's people.* All believers are one in Christ. Though drawn from every segment of humanity, they make up one vast family, one redeemed people, one spiritual temple. They share equally in the privileges and blessings of the gospel.

FOR FURTHER STUDY

1. Consider the significance for us of Paul's discussion of the relationship between Jews and Gentiles.

2. Using a concordance, study the New Testament references to "cross," "blood," "peace," "reconcile," "access," etc.

CHAPTER 7

Paul's Special Mission in Regard to God's New People

(Ephesians 3:1-21)

This chapter, the most intensely personal section of the Ephesian Epistle, consists of a prayer (vss. 1, 14-21) that is interrupted by a long digression (vss. 2-13). The digression, which forms an extended interpretation of Paul's special ministry to the Gentiles, is really the heart of the chapter. It is a sort of explanatory parenthesis that Paul must have felt was essential to the full appreciation of the prayer he had on his heart for his readers. Beare calls it "one of the most important passages of the entire epistle, both in the soaring flights of its thought and in the corresponding magnificence of its expression" (p. 664). Much of it is in the form of a personal testimony, but the statement of this leads the apostle to make far-reaching declarations about the church — both as to the equality of its members before God (vss. 6, 8, 9) and as to its place in the eternal plan of God (vss. 10-12).

I. AN EXPLANATION OF PAUL'S SPECIAL MISSION (3:1-13)

The opening words of chapter 3 appear to be the approach to a statement about prayer. The thought, however, is abruptly broken off and is not resumed until verse 14 is reached. (Some modern translations, for example ASV and RSV, show the broken construction by placing a dash at the end of verse 1. The verb for the verse is perhaps to be supplied from verse 14. See Knox's translation.)

"For this cause" (vs. 1) points back to the thought set forth in the last half of chapter 2. More specifically, the words refer to the last verse of that chapter, in which Paul declared that his readers were being built into a habitation for God. It was contemplation of the wonder of this that moved the apostle to prayer for his readers.

Paul describes himself as "a prisoner for Christ Jesus on behalf of you Gentiles" (vs. 1b, RSV). "Prisoner" is to be taken literally, an indication that the apostle was in prison at the time of writing this letter. (See the discussion of his imprisonment in the "Introduction.") "On behalf of you Gentiles" (Goodspeed, "for the sake of you heathen") points up that Paul felt it was his work in the interest of and among the Gentiles that had led to his arrest and imprisonment (cf. 21:27ff.; 23:21,22). That he was a "prisoner for Christ Jesus" on behalf of the Gentiles suggests Paul's awareness that a special work among the Gentiles had been assigned him by Christ (cf. Acts 23:12-21). It was not a work of his own choosing but a commission received from the living Lord.

Paul's mention of his appointed ministry to the Gentiles (vs. 1) leads him to consider in greater detail its nature (vss. 2-7,13) and purpose (vss. 8-13).[1] (Observe how in this chapter he repeatedly relates his work to the Gentiles, particularly in vss. 1,2,8,13.)

1. *The Nature of Paul's Mission* (vss. 2-7,13). Paul was confident that his readers had some awareness of his unique mission in the work of the gospel (vs. 2: "assuming that you have heard, etc.," RSV). Yet he felt it necessary to remind them of his ministry and to explain in some detail its significance. The various ideas expressed may be summed up under three words: stewardship (vss. 2-6), service (vss. 7-12), and suffering (vs. 13).

(1) Stewardship (vss. 2-6). According to the reading of KJV, Paul describes his work as a "dispensation of the grace of God which is given me to you-ward" (vs. 2). The word "dispensation," the term used in KJV, denotes an arrangement or a plan; it says nothing specifically about the nature of Paul's work, but rather points up the mode in which he had been selected for it. That is, this rendering suggests that Paul's ministry was not of his own choosing but was the result of an arrangement or plan by which the grace of God was given to him. (Cf. NEB, "Surely you have heard how God has assigned the gift of his grace to me for your benefit.") The Greek word employed by Paul may have this meaning, but that is not its primary significance. It was used in New Testament times of the office and function of a steward, one trusted with the management of another's property (cf. Luke 16:2-4). Indeed, its literal meaning is "management of a household." In the present context it is best rendered by our word *stewardship* (cf. RSV). Paul's use of it here shows that he conceived of his position as both a high privilege and a sacred trust (cf. 1 Cor. 9:17; Col. 1:25).

Three things are said about this stewardship. First, it concerned the "grace of God" (vs. 2). The word "grace" is used here in its widest significance for the whole concept of divine favor. To speak of a "stewardship" of grace is to acknowledge that God's favor is not given as a luxury to be privately enjoyed, but as a boon to be joyfully shared with others (cf. 1 Peter 4:10).

---

[1]This entire passage should be read alongside Colossians 1:24-29.

Second, Paul's stewardship of grace had particular reference to his Gentile readers ("to you-ward," vs. 2). God's house (2:20-22) is composed of the redeemed from various racial groups, but Paul felt it was his special function to build the Gentile portion of that house.

Third, this stewardship involved a great "mystery" of redemption (vss. 3-6). We have seen that in the New Testament a mystery is something previously concealed but now made known in the gospel. In 1:9 "mystery" spoke of God's purpose of gathering together all things under the headship of Christ. Here it refers to one phase of that ultimate goal, namely, the inclusion of Gentiles in the blessings of the gospel and the terms on which this is done.

Paul claims (vss. 3b, 4) to have a special knowledge of the purpose of God for the Gentiles. Enough had been written (cf. 1:9-11; 2:11-22) to make this obvious to his readers. How the apostle came to have his understanding of the divine mystery is also explained. It was not by research, not by rationalizing, not by human instruction, but "by revelation" from God. This does not necessarily mean that a full comprehension of the mystery came in a single dramatic experience (though that is a possible interpretation). More likely, it was a gradual unfolding of the divine plan that spanned a good many years of the apostle's life. Perhaps he had especially in mind that time spent in Arabia shortly after his conversion (Gal. 1:11-18). No doubt the long period of imprisonment, during which Ephesians was written, afforded time for a deepening of his comprehension of this great purpose of God. At any rate, Paul's grasp of the matter came directly from God, not through men.

Verse 5 tells of the public manifestation of the mystery (hidden purpose or secret) of God. This greatest of all secrets remained undisclosed for ages. In past generations, writes Paul, it was "not made known unto the sons of men, as it is now revealed unto his holy apostles and prophets by the Spirit." The stress falls on the word "as," the thought being that the mystery had not been made known with the fullness and clarity that it has now. That Gentiles were included in God's purpose was, in a way, known in Old Testament times. Even to Abraham it was said, "In thee shall all families of the earth be blessed" (Gen. 12:3). But what was not fully comprehended in Old Testament times was that God would deal with Jews and Gentiles alike on the common ground of grace.

It is just this point that Paul emphasizes in verse 6, where he gives the content of the mystery of Christ: "that the Gentiles are fellow-heirs and fellow-members of the body, and fellow-partakers of the promise in Christ Jesus through the gospel" (ASV). Note the repetition of the word *fellow*. Its reiteration is the key to the meaning and significance of the verse. Gentiles, upon entering God's kingdom, share equally in all its blessings. They are not second-class citizens; they are "fellow-heirs" in relation to Jewish believers, "fellow-members" in relation to the body of Christ, and "fellow-partakers" in relation to the messianic promise. God now wants all people to know this great gospel secret.

It is "by the gospel" that Gentiles — and indeed all races of men — come into this happy relationship. "Hence the urgency," said W. O. Carver, "for preaching the gospel to 'the whole creation,' to 'all nations,' to 'every man.' All men must be given the knowledge of the Christ because they are all equally offered the blessings of God in him" (p. 131).

(2) Service (vss. 7-12). In verses 2-6 we have seen how God revealed the secret that Gentiles are included equally with Jews in His purpose of grace. Paul interpreted his relation to this purpose in terms of stewardship. The apostle moves one step beyond this idea in verse 7. Here he declares that God had made him a "minister" of the good news of salvation by which the Gentiles were actually to be brought in. That is to say, Paul's stewardship was carried out in the service of the gospel. The Greek word for "minister" (*diakonos*), meaning servant or attendant, is the word from which we get our word *deacon*. Here it denotes one who serves in the interest of, and for the benefit of, another. The word itself is used in the New Testament in reference to the apostles and their helpers (for example, 2 Cor. 6:4; 1 Tim. 4:6). It is used of Phoebe (Rom. 1:16). It is used of Christ (Rom. 15:8). It is even used of the servants of Satan (2 Cor. 11:15). Christ used the verb form when he said, "I am among you as *he that serveth*" (Luke 22:27) and, "For even the Son of man came not *to be ministered* unto, but *to minister*" (Mark 10:45).

The preceding verses have pulsated with Paul's wonder at the inclusion of the Gentiles in God's plan of redemption. Verses 7-12 show his profound gratitude for the privilege of making this fact known to them. When Paul says he was "made" a minister (vs. 7), he indicates that he did not take this honor to himself; he was divinely appointed to his office. It was this vivid sense of a divine call that led Paul to write in another place, "Necessity is laid upon me; for woe is unto me, if I preach not the gospel" (1 Cor. 9:16), ASV).

The apostle looked on this appointment to ministry in two ways. First, it was a great favor. He was not made a minister in consideration of any worthiness or merit within himself, but rather "according to the gift of [consisting in] the grace of God" (vs. 7). The sense of privilege and gratitude expressed by these words is all the more remarkable when we recall that Paul's ministry to the Gentiles had cost him dearly. The bitter hatred of his countrymen, the contempt of many of those he sought to win, the privations and perils of his journeys, the indignity and pain of stoning, whippings, imprisonment — these things were part of the price

Paul paid for preaching. Even while he wrote these words, he was bound with a chain to a Roman soldier and for all he knew would never be a free man again. But all that Paul could say was, "The service of Christ is an unspeakable privilege. It is an expression of the favor of God."

Second, Paul saw his introduction into the ministry as involving the exercise of divine power. He was made a minister "by [according to, in proportion to] the effectual working of his [God's] power" (vs. 7). The primary reference is to Paul's induction into the office of apostle. His apostleship was to him nothing less than the result of the working of the omnipotence of God. His words recall the scene on the Damascus road, with its blazing light outshining the noonday sun. Here, to be sure, was grace unspeakable, but here also was limitless power.

Perhaps also there is in these words a reference to the efficacy of Paul's ministry, the suggestion being that this was dependent not on his own natural capacities but on the working of God's power. Preaching to a pagan world required such power.

"Effectual working" translates a Greek word from which we get our word *energy*. In the New Testament it is used almost exclusively for the inworking of divine power. Here it might be rendered "energizing strength" or "active energy" (cf. 1:19). The word for "power" is the one from which we get such words as "dynamic," "dynamite," "dynamo," and so on. The force behind Paul's apostolic labors was thus declared to be the active strength of the dynamic power of God.

(3) Suffering (vs. 13). Paul not only saw his work as a stewardship of grace and as a service in the gospel by which the Gentiles were being brought into God's redemptive purpose; he also interpreted it in terms of suffering. He knew from experience that the way of service is not always an easy way. For him the calling of God meant "blood, sweat, and tears." Read the catalog of his trials in 2 Corinthians 11:23-28. Indeed, even as he wrote this letter, there dangled from his body a chain that bound him twenty-four hours a day to a Roman soldier.

The word translated "tribulations" literally means "pressure" but is used in the Bible in the sense of affliction or tribulation. Generally it connotes affliction or tribulation that is intense and protracted. Paul's afflictions, he tells his Gentile readers, are "for you" (vs. 13). The sufferings were incurred in their interest, in the carrying out of his mission in their behalf (cf. Col. 1:24).[2]

2. *The Purpose of Paul's Mission* (vss. 8-13). Paul magnified the dignity of his office, but he was always possessed with a sense of his own personal unworthiness. "Unto me [the pronoun is emphatic], who am

---

[2]For further discussion of this verse see the second from the last paragraph of the following section.

less than the least of all saints, is this grace given" (vs. 8). "There can be no doubt," writes Charles Brown, "that preaching to the Gentiles would have been regarded by some of Paul's contemporaries in the Christian Church as the greatest humiliation of their lives; to him it was the highest honour, a grace and a gift that he welcomed with grateful and adoring heart" (pp. 69,70).

The Greek word rendered "less than the least" is a most unusual one, found only in this passage. It is really a superlative form to which Paul added a comparative ending; "leaster," if there were such a word, would be the meaning. It was not enough for Paul to use a word that meant "least"; he wanted a place beneath the least. One thinks of the old Puritan who said, "I do not quarrel with Paul's language, but I do dispute his right to push me out of my place. Less than the least," said he, "is my place."

The "grace" (vs. 8) refers to Paul's office, his apostleship. The TCNT renders the whole phrase, "to me . . . was this *charge* entrusted" (italics mine). Having called attention to it, he proceeds to state a threefold purpose God had in calling him to the apostolic office.

(1) A missionary purpose (vs. 8). God's intention was that Paul "should preach among the Gentiles the unsearchable riches of Christ." The entire statement is deeply meaningful. In the Greek, "Gentiles" is emphatic by its position. It was Paul's unique ministry in relation to them that still occupied his mind and filled his heart with wonder. To him it was a high and thrilling privilege to proclaim that the Messiah promised to the Jews is Savior of the Gentiles also. From the word for "preach," which means "to announce glad tidings," our word "evangelize" is derived.

Most suggestive is Paul's description of his message as "the unsearchable riches of Christ." The phrase brings to mind the boundless resources in Christ for meeting the needs of sinful humanity. These resources, Paul declares, are "unsearchable." This vivid word, meaning literally "untrackable" or "inexplorable," denotes that which is too vast to be measured. Its use here projects a sense of wonder and amazement.

> It suggests the figure of a man standing, with uplifted hands, in a posture of great amazement, before continuous revelations of immeasurable and unspeakable glory. . . . It is as if a man were tracking out the confines of a lake, walking its boundaries, and when the circuit were almost complete should discover that it was no lake at all, but an arm of the ocean, and he was confronted by the immeasurable sea! (Jowett, pp. 9,10).

The word is found elsewhere in the New Testament only in Romans 11:33. There it is used of the ways and purposes of God and suggests that which is unfathomable, beyond human comprehension.

(2) A didactic purpose (vs. 9). A second purpose of Paul's ministry was "to make all men see what is the dispensation[3] of the mystery" (ASV) (cf. RSV, the plan[4] of the mystery"[5]). The thought concerns the worldwide distribution of the news and blessings of the gospel and the manner in which God intends this to be done. The chief thing, however, concerns Paul's relation to all this. God's intention had always been to offer a redemption of worldwide application, but for all practical purposes that intention lay unrevealed in his own bosom until in the gospel it was made an open secret. The stewardship (or administration, or plan) of the secret, the particular manner in which God would convey and apply it to the world at large was for Paul to make known. Cf. NEB, "To me . . . he has granted . . . the privilege . . . of bringing to light how this hidden purpose was to be put into effect."

The apostle depicts himself as a teacher whose task it is to bring out the profound implications of the gospel. God particularly wanted him to help all men see the worldwide scope of the gospel and to make clear the plan by which God intends to get out to all men the secret of His love for the world. "It was — and is — necessary that the divine method for dispensing this glorious good news shall be known and accepted, known to all and accepted as the duty and glory of all Christians. Alas, that they have been so little concerned with it" (Carver, p. 132).

Actually, the clause under consideration is very closely related to the one discussed in the preceding verse, for it was by preaching to the Gentiles the unsearchable riches of Christ that the mystery of redemption was made manifest to the world. Preaching the gospel to the Gentiles, says Lenski, "was like setting the deep mystery into the fullest light of day so that all men might see it" (pp. 477,478).

(3) An ultimate purpose (vss. 10-13). Most of us, even from the vantage point of the twentieth century, have a very limited concept of the breadth, the grandeur, the infinite range of God's purpose of grace. Something of the magnitude and completeness of that purpose is suggested by verses 10,11. Here Paul states the ultimate aim of his preaching the gospel to the Gentiles and of his enlightening all men regarding the stewardship (or plan) of a world-embracing redemption. It is all "to the intent that now unto the principalities and powers in heavenly places might be known by the church the manifold wisdom of God" (vs. 10). Phillips: "The purpose is that all the angelic powers should now see the complex wisdom of God's plan being worked out through the Church."

Notice that the recipients of this new knowledge are "the prin-

---

[3]Greek *oikonomia*.
[4]Greek, *oikonomia* (cf. 1:10; 3:2).
[5]See 1:9; 3:3-6 for a discussion of "mystery."

cipalities and powers in heavenly places." "Principalities" and "powers" refer to various ranks and orders of angelic beings (cf. Eph. 1:21). That angelic beings are intensely interested in human redemption is clear from 1 Peter 1:12. Here we are told that their knowledge and blessedness are increased by the exhibition of the work of God in the salvation of men.

Again, observe that what they learn concerns not the love or power of God but "the manifold wisdom of God." Cf. NEB, "the wisdom of God in all its varied forms." Peter writes of God's "manifold grace" (1 Peter 4:10), but the adjective he uses is not exactly the same as the one employed here. Paul's word for "manifold," found only here in the New Testament, is an especially vivid one, literally meaning "many-colored." There may be in the word an allusion to the intricate beauty of an embroidered pattern. In this text the word probably suggests both beauty and diversity.

It seems that the wisdom of God is especially mentioned in reference to the complicated problem of human redemption and, more particularly, the plan for the proclamation of that redemption on a worldwide scale. Eadie eloquently states that angelic beings

> have seen much of God's working — many a sun lighted up, and many a world launched into its orbit. They have been delighted with the solution of many a problem, and the development of many a mystery. But in the proclamation of the gospel to the Gentiles, . . . involving the origination and the extinction of Judaism, the incarnation and the atonement, the manger and the cross . . . these "principalities and powers in heavenly places" beheld with rapture other and brighter phases of a wisdom which had often dazzled them by its brilliant and profuse versatility (p. 234).

The special instrument of instruction to these heavenly beings is "the church,"[6] referred to here in its broadest significance as made up of the whole body of redeemed people. The chief point is that the very existence of the church, uniting hostile sections of mankind in one body, is an obvious proof that God is gathering up all creation in Christ. The church is thus viewed as the visible materialization of the purpose of God for the universe. Angelic beings behold it with wonder, and as they see in it the purpose of God taking shape, they gain enlarged insight into the wonderful wisdom of God.

All of this, Paul adds, was "according to the eternal purpose which God purposed in Christ Jesus our Lord" (vs. 11). Cf. RSV, ". . . which he has realized in Christ Jesus our Lord." The idea is that the use of the church to make known the all-embracing wisdom of God was no after-

---

[6]Findlay fittingly entitles his exposition of this passage "Earth Teaching Heaven" (George G. Findlay, *Epistle to the Ephesians*. The Expositor's Bible, ed. W. Robertson Nicoll. [London: Hodder and Stoughton, n.d.]).

thought with Him. The church's role in the scheme of redemption was always a part of His plan. And that plan has now been achieved in "Christ Jesus our Lord."

Verse 12 shows that the Christ through whom God's eternal purpose is accomplished is none other than the Jesus known by Christians, and through union with whom they "have boldness and access with confidence by the faith of [i.e., through faith in] him." "The same Lord who is the stay of our faith and hope is also the crown of the whole development of the world" (Westcott, p. 129).

Note the three leading words of verse 12: *boldness, access, confidence.* All this we have in Christ. "Boldness," suggesting absence of restraint or fear, translates a Greek word that literally denotes freedom of speech. It was used in classical Greek of the free speech that was the right of every citizen of a democratic state. In the New Testament it signifies the liberty of believers to approach God directly through Christ, with the added notion of freedom from the fear of being rejected. "Access," which betokens approach to God (cf. 2:18), is the principal word here. "Confidence" suggests assurance of acceptance. The three words are bound together so as to form one complete idea, namely, that through faith in Christ we have free, unrestricted, confident access to God. The TCNT brings out the meaning: "In union with him [Christ], and through our trust in him, we find courage to approach God with confidence."

The long parenthesis begun at verse 2 is concluded in verse 13. The thought of this verse is as follows: The Ephesians must not let Paul's afflictions cause them to lose heart, but instead must look upon them as an occasion for glorifying God. True, the champion of Gentile evangelization may be in fetters, but the Word of God is not bound. His purpose of worldwide redemption will be worked out in spite of Paul's imprisonment. Indeed, Paul's very willingness to suffer on behalf of the Gentiles was itself an indication of God's favor toward them.

"Wherefore" refers to all that Paul said in verses 2-12 about the nature and dignity of his office as apostle to the Gentiles and its significance for the Ephesians. The Greek word for "faint" means to lose heart, to become discouraged. Paul did not want his readers to lose heart concerning the great cause of Gentile evangelization. His imprisonment did not mean that God's purpose was frustrated. Nor did his afflictions mean that he was out of the path of duty. Indeed, his sufferings were the direct consequence of his obedience to, and participation in, the eternal purpose of God for the redemption of the race. The readers, instead of being discouraged at Paul's afflictions, should glory in them, for they were an evidence that God's purpose of grace was advancing toward its consummation.

Before proceeding to consider the remainder of this chapter, one would do well to ponder some of the concepts and impressions conveyed by the first thirteen verses. Look carefully at the heart of Paul as it is laid bare in the passage — his unworthiness, his appreciation of the greatness of his work, and his sense of wonder at the message of redemption. Again, consider the marvelous scope of God's redemptive purpose, the unique task that God's people have in relation to that purpose, and how full and wonderful is the gospel of grace.

II. A Prayer Occasioned by Contemplation of Paul's Mission and Message (3:1, 14-21)

Following the parenthesis in verses 2-13, Paul gets back to his prayer, begun in verse 1. Perhaps it was the mention of the believer's confidence in approaching God (vs. 12) that turned his thinking again to an expression of prayerful concern for his readers. At any rate, he here gives utterance to his deepest desires for them.

One would think that Paul in his lonely imprisonment had burdens enough of his own without thinking of the needs of people far removed from the place of his confinement. Some of these people he had never seen, but he gathered them up in his prayers and pleaded with God on their behalf.

The prayer contained in our text is generally acknowledged to be the most sublime, the most far-reaching, and the most majestic prayer found anywhere in Paul's Epistles, or possibly in the whole Bible. Compared with it, much that passes for prayer in our experience is hardly deserving of the name.

But this is more than just a noble prayer. Written under divine inspiration, it reveals not only the requests of Paul for the Ephesians but also the desire and longing of God for all of His people. It is an expression of His purpose, a statement of the ultimate goal of redemption that He intends His people to realize.

1. *The Approach to the Prayer* (vss. 14,15). "For this cause" (vs. 14) suggests the reason for the prayer and resumes the line of thought interrupted by the parenthesis of verses 2-13. It points in a general way to the teaching of 2:11-22 concerning all that God has wrought in Christ for the Gentiles. More particularly, it refers to those aspects of the divine purpose set forth in 3:2-13. Paul's prayer, therefore, was offered because of his deep interest in the people of God, because of his sincere desire that his Gentile readers might enter fully into their privileges in Christ.

The customary posture in prayer among the Jews was that of standing (cf. Mark 11:25; Luke 18:11,13); a kneeling position betokened special solemnity or unusual urgency (cf. Luke 22:41; Acts 7:60). With us it is much the same. Sometimes one may close his eyes and lift his heart in prayer to God while sitting quietly in a favorite chair. Sometimes, as in our services of public worship, we may engage in prayer while standing. But there are other times when there is such intense earnestness, such an overwhelming burden, that one finds himself irresistibly forced to his knees. Therefore, when Paul says, "I bow my knees," the words are indicative of the intense earnestness and the unusual emotion he felt. It may be that as the apostle dictated his letter he instinctively dropped to his knees at this point and gave utterance to his prayer.

The prayer is addressed to "the Father of our Lord Jesus Christ, of whom the whole family in heaven and earth is named" (vss. 14,15). The words translated by "of our Lord Jesus Christ" are not in the best manuscripts and are accordingly omitted from modern translations. "Father" therefore is used absolutely, as the name by which God is invoked in prayer (cf. 2:18). Paul was thinking not so much of God's relation to Christ as of His relation to His redeemed people. The use of the word in this context points up the loving confidence and assurance with which Paul approached the throne of grace.

In verse 15 Paul gives a further description of God. He is the One "of whom the whole family in heaven and earth is named." Goodspeed has "from whom every family in heaven or on earth takes its name." "Family" is used in the sense of clan, tribe, or nation — any group that claims descent from a common ancestor (father). If we follow the KJV rendering, the expression "whole family" should probably be taken as a reference to the company of the redeemed both in heaven and on earth, the thought being that they make up one great family, with God as their Father. The following words express the thought:

> Let saints on earth unite to sing
>   With those to glory gone;
> For all the servants of our King,
>   In earth and heaven, are one.
> One family we dwell in him,
>   One Church above, beneath;
> Though now divided by the stream,
>   The narrow stream of death.

—Author unknown

If we follow the rendering of ASV, Goodspeed, RSV, and others ("every family"), the reference seems to be to the various classes and groupings of men on earth and of angels in heaven. That is to say, this interpretation suggests that every group of intelligent beings, whether in heaven or on earth, gets the name "family" from the one Father. They are all related to God, and it is only in virtue of that relation that any of them has the name "family." Westcott, commenting on the words "in heaven and earth," writes, "He who is the Father of men is also the source of fellowship and unity in all the orders of finite beings."

There is a play on words in the Greek that unfortunately cannot be adequately expressed in an English translation, for the Greek word for "family" (*patria*) is built on the same root as the word for "father" (*pater*). The thought may be partly expressed thus: "I bow my knees to the Father from whom all fatherhood is named" (i.e., derives its name and nature).

The fatherhood of God is not merely a metaphor drawn from human relationships. The converse is true. He is the fountain of fatherhood and all fatherliness. The original, archetypal fatherhood is God's; all others are in some sense derived from Him. The human relationship is only a reflection of which the divine fatherhood is the reality. Well does Bruce say that "the more nearly any fatherhood, natural or spiritual, approaches in character to God's perfect fatherhood, the more truly does it manifest fatherhood as God intended it to be" (p. 67).

2. *The Boldness of the Prayer* (vs. 16a). Paul's desire is that God may grant his requests "according to [on the pattern of] the riches of his glory." He had in mind the limitless resources of God, and he is asking that his readers may receive the benefits they require in accordance with God's ability to give. Sometimes we seem to be fearful lest we should ask too much of God. We approach Him timidly, as though we were not sure He could meet our needs. Let us learn from Paul's inspired prayer that we can never strain the resources of God. He does not give grudgingly nor in meager portions, as if he were afraid he might exhaust his wealth. He gives according to the measure of his infinite fullness, as John Newton has so well said:

> Thou art coming to a King;
> Large petitions with thee bring;
> For his grace and power are such,
> None can ever ask too much.

3. *The Contents of the Prayer* (vss. 16b-18). Opinions differ as to the number of requests in this prayer, but the Greek text lends support to the view that there are three principal petitions, each being introduced by the same Greek conjunction (*hina*). They are progressive, however, rather than coordinate. That is to say, they are like the steps of a ladder, each moving higher but being built on what has gone before. Closely knit, with thought melting into thought, they "open out one into the other like some majestic suite of apartments in a great palace-temple, each leading into a loftier and more spacious hall, each drawing nearer the presence-chamber, until at last we stand there" (Maclaren, p. 132). The climax of the prayer is reached in the closing words of verse 19: "that

ye might be filled with all the fulness of God."

(1) A request for inner power (vss. 16,17a). The first request, for inner power, is contained in the words, "that he would grant you . . . to be strengthened with might by his Spirit in the inner man; [so] that Christ may dwell in your heart by faith." The words speak of a strengthening that is effected by the impartation of divine power. This strengthening takes place "in the inner man," which is that part of our being that includes the mind, the will, the conscience, and so on — in short, the seat of intellectual and spiritual life. Paul used the same phrase in 2 Corinthians 4:1b. There it is contrasted with the "outward man," which obviously is a reference to the physical side of man's life. Weymouth therefore understands "the inner man" to mean "your inmost being." Beare speaks of "the inner man" as referring in Pauline usage to "the highest part of our nature" (p. 677). In Romans 7:22 Paul refers to it as the part of being by which Christians delight in the law of God. In 2 Corinthians 4:16,18 the inner man is said to be renewed day by day.

Blaikie reminds us that "faith, trust, humility, love, patience, and the like graces" belong to the inner man. These, he explains, "are what we are weakest in, and what we have least power to make strong" (p. 108).

"That Christ may dwell in your hearts" may be thought of as a further definition of the inward strengthening. Or, more likely, the words may suggest the issue and result of such divine strengthening. Either way, Paul is not referring to the coming of Christ into the heart at conversion. The persons in behalf of whom this supplication was originally made were already believers and in a true sense indwelt by the living Christ. What Paul desired was that Christ's presence in them might be both real and regnant. Graham Scroggie explains that Christ's

> presence in us has its degrees and advances, its less and more, its outer and inner. A life may be truly Christian and yet far from fully Christian. It is this which distinguishes one Christian from another. Some have made little room for Christ, some give Him more, and in some He has the whole house. Or, viewed from another standpoint, in.some Christ is just present, in others He is prominent, and in others again, He is preeminent (p. 70).

(2) A request for comprehension (vss. 17b-19a). The second petition, "that ye . . . may be able to comprehend . . . and to know the love of Christ," grows out of the first. In a general sense it is a prayer that believers, as a consequence of the divine strengthening and indwelling, may have spiritual capacity for understanding the love of Christ.

The thought of the petition revolves around two phrases: "to comprehend" (vs. 18) and "to know" (vs. 19). The first betokens a mental grasp and might better be rendered by the word "apprehend." The idea is of laying hold on something so as to make it one's own. The word for "know" represents knowledge gained by experience. Thus, the prayer is that Christians may with their minds lay hold on Christ's love and in their personal experience come to have a true and enlarging experience of it.[7]

There are three conditions to this knowledge, and each one suggests that it involves far more than intellectual action. First, one must himself be "rooted [like a deeply planted tree] and grounded [like a well-founded building] in love" (vs. 17b). The thought is of a firm and constant love that goes out to both God and our fellowman.

Second, one must be endowed with God's power. This is suggested by the words "be able" (vs. 18). They translate a Greek word that means to be mighty, to be eminently able, to have full capacity. As in all other spiritual endeavors, our sufficiency for apprehending Christ's love must come from God.

Third, one must pursue the knowledge of this love together with all saints (vs. 18a). Isolation from other believers is a barrier to the kind of comprehension Paul had in mind. It is not as a matter of private experience but in fellowship with all the family of God that we explore the measureless reaches of His love. God has so ordered things that those who love the company of His people are in the best position to grasp the richness of His love. This is one thing that makes public worship so important. The experiences of our fellow believers are intended to be (and usually will be) of help to us in our own fuller realization of Christ and His love.

The reference to the dimensions of Christ's love — its breadth, and length, and depth, and height (vs. 18) — is intended to bring out the all-encompassing character of that love. The imagination of interpreters has run riot in the endeavor to find some distinctive, spiritual meaning in each of these four words. Some, for example, see in the terms a reference to the fact that Christ's love is as broad as the human race, as long as eternity, as deep as human misery and sin, and as high as heaven. Paul probably did not have anything this specific in mind. The accumulation of words was meant simply to suggest the surpassing magnitude of Christ's love for men.

"Which passeth knowledge" has been called "the fifth dimension"

---

[7]The object we are to apprehend is not specifically stated; only the dimensions of it are given — "the breadth, and length, and depth, and height." Most interpreters think the object of comprehension is "the love of Christ" (vs. 19), and that is the interpretation preferred here. Some interpreters, however, understand "the breadth, and length, and depth, etc." to refer to the divine purpose rather than to the love of Christ (cf. Beare, p. 679). Others understand a reference to the vastness and glory of that spiritual temple described in the closing verses of chapter 2 (cf. Blaikie, p. 108).

of the love of Christ. The words mean that His love for us is too great ever to be fully known. "We know, and know deeply, increasingly, blessedly, and yet all the while there are infinite stretches of love beyond our highest experiences" (Griffith Thomas, p. 122).

> For the love of God is broader
>   Than the measure of man's mind;
> And the heart of the Eternal
>   Is most wonderfully kind.

— Frederick W. Faber

(3) A request for the fullness of God (vs. 19b). The final petition, the climax of the entire prayer, is a request for believers to "be filled with [up to the measure] all the fulness of God."[8] No prayer can possibly reach beyond this, for in this filling every other blessing is included. The full meaning of it is beyond our comprehension, but in a general way it may be seen as a prayer that the Ephesian Christians may be filled with all spiritual excellence. Perhaps it is stated in terms of an ideal, somewhat like Jesus' injunction to be perfect as our Father in heaven is perfect (Matt. 5:48).

To interpret more specifically, attention must be focused on the phrase "the fulness of God." This seems to be an expression standing for the sum total of all the energies, powers, and attributes of God (cf. Col. 1:19; 2:9). Of course Paul does not mean to suggest that mortal man can ever contain within himself the fullness of the divine essence, and we must guard against so interpreting his words. Solomon long before had declared that "heaven and the heaven of heavens cannot contain" God (2 Chron. 6:18). What then is the import of Paul's words? His prayer is that his readers may experience to the extent of their capacity the totality of blessings God is willing and able to bestow. That is to say, he is requesting that their whole being may be filled with God's presence and power, so that there shall be no room for more — like the teacup on the seashore filled to overflowing with the swelling water of the vast ocean. This is the issue of all that has been requested earlier in the prayer — the strengthening by the Spirit, the full realization of the indwelling Christ, the experiential knowledge of the love of Christ. All of these lead to and culminate in the fullness of God in the Christian life.

This petition staggers the imagination, but we must not let its magnitude cause us to set it aside as an impossibility. Indeed, every believer already knows something of this experience, for "of his [Christ's] fulness have all we received, and grace for grace" (John 1:16). And in another part of this Epistle Paul sets before us the goal of growing

---

[8]Observe how the petitions of this great prayer cluster around the three Persons of the Godhead: Spirit (vs. 16), Christ (vss. 17,19a), God (vs. 19b).

"unto the measure of the stature of the fulness of Christ" (Eph. 4:13). In light of this overwhelming conception, we should take Paul's prayer not only as an expression of God's desire and purpose, but also as a promise that in its fullest sense it will one day come to pass.[9]

Scroggie sums up the three petitions in this manner:

> By the strengthening of the Spirit Christ will come to dwell more largely and richly in our hearts, and this double blessing will result in a fuller apprehension and knowledge of the love of God in Christ, and all this will have for its issue our being ever more completely "filled into the fulness of God" (pp. 177,178).

4. *The Conclusion to the Prayer* (vss. 20,21). Paul closed his prayer with a lofty doxology. These verses, however, are more than the conclusion of the prayer. They are really the grand climax of all that has been set forth in chapters 1-3 about God's purpose and our redemption. They assure us that God is abundantly able to carry out His plans.

Verse 20, which speaks of the inconceivable greatness of the power of God, expresses Paul's confidence in God to meet our every need. As comprehensive as the apostle's requests are, they are more than matched by God's power to answer them. William Carey's motto, "Expect great things from God," catches the spirit of this verse.

In using the words "exceeding abundantly above all that we ask or think," Paul was laboring to express the boundless reach of God's power. It exceeds all our requests; it exceeds even our highest thoughts — and this "exceeding abundantly." How wonderful it is that we who cannot begin even to comprehend God's power are yet privileged to be the earthly instruments through whom His power operates.

"The power that worketh in us" is described in Ephesians 1:19ff. There we learn that it brought Christ from the grave and raised us from spiritual death. Such power can subdue within us all our base passions and make possible the achievement of every worthy and noble goal in life. There is a hint here that the only limitation on God's power is our willingness to permit Him to work in us freely.

Verse 21 is an ascription of glory to God. Glory belongs inherently to Him; it is His exclusive prerogative. It is our responsibility to acknowledge it, reflect it, and make it known. The word is very broad in its meaning and therefore is not always easy to define. As a general rule, it denotes God's majesty and splendor. Here, however, it seems to shade off into the idea of praise.

The chapter closes with a reference to the church as the sphere within which the glory of God is exhibited. The suggestion is that the

---

[9]A number of interpreters feel that the "ye" (vss. 17,19) is collective. They understand Paul to be pleading for something that pertains to the whole body of Christ, not Christians as individuals.

glory of God is the very reason for the church's existence. As the Westminster Catechism puts it, "Man's chief end is to glorify God, and to enjoy him forever." We can add nothing to the inherent glory of God, but we can so live as to enable others to see His glory.

SUMMARY

The section of Scripture that we have been considering contains a wondrously rich vein of spiritual truth. The study of it should impress at least the following things upon our minds:

1. *The Privilege of Sharing in the Redemptive Plan of God.* This plan, which concerns the worldwide distribution of the gospel, has been in the mind of God from eternity. Many people have the impression that salvation was offered to the Gentiles only because the Jews rejected it. We learn from this passage that God's purpose from the beginning was for men of all races to share alike in the salvation provided in Jesus Christ.

The all-embracing scope of God's purpose, however, was not fully revealed until apostolic times. It was faintly known by some of the spiritual giants of Israel. But, generally speaking, it was a secret hidden to men who lived before Christ came into the world.

Now, the situation is different. The secret is out. We know that salvation is not limited to those of one race or of one part of the globe. We have no excuse, therefore, if we are not actively engaged in telling this good news to every creature.

2. *The Need for Great Praying.* We need to enlarge our spiritual desires and stretch our confidence in God's power to grant them. What we receive from Him is limited, not by His ability, but by the smallness of our requests. God has rich treasures for us, but we must reach for them. Alexander Maclaren pointed out that "we may have as much of God as we can hold, as much as we wish. All Niagara may roar past a man's door, but only as much as he diverts through his own sluice will drive his mill, or quench his thirst" (p. 189).

3. *The Primacy of Character.* It is instructive to note that when Paul thought of the needs of the people to whom he addressed this letter, he did not make mention of anything physical or material. It surely was not because his readers had no need of material benefits. The truth is that many of them were likely in dire poverty.

Paul, however, felt that the matter of paramount concern about a Christian is his spiritual condition. Therefore, the things mentioned in his prayer all have to do with the inner life, with the cultivation of true Christian character. We may need to be reminded from time to time that what we are is more basic than what we do, for what we are will inevitably determine what we do.

4. *The Church as a Channel for Glorifying God.* Think of the ways by which you and your church may best express the glory of God in a world that is blind to that glory (cf. 1 Peter 2:9,10).

FOR FURTHER STUDY

1. Using a concordance, study the uses of the words *mystery, dispensation, riches, full, fullness,* etc.

2. Write out in your own words the petitions of Ephesians 3:14-21.

3. Begin to make a list of all of the teachings of Ephesians about the church.

4. Read "The Unsearchable Riches of Christ" in Spurgeon's *Treasury of the Bible: New Testament.* Maclaren's *Expositions of Holy Scripture* contains seven sermons on chapter 3. See especially "The Climax of All Prayer."

CHAPTER 8

The Daily Walk of God's New People: Spiritual Obligations

(Ephesians 4:1-16)

To facilitate our study of Ephesians, we have broken up the text into eleven sections. The Epistle may be seen, however, as composed of only two *major* divisions. One is distinctly doctrinal (chs. 1-3), and the other is mainly practical or hortatory (chs. 4-6). The former section, which is cast in the form of a devotional meditation, consists in the main of an exposition of the redemptive purpose of God and the place of the church in that purpose. In the latter section (chs. 4-6) the apostle brings out the ethical implications of his doctrine and urges the readers to put them into practice.

The pivotal verse of the whole Epistle — indeed, the key that unlocks its structure — may be said to be 4:1. It gathers up in a single phrase ("the vocation wherewith ye are called") the theme of chapters 1-3, and in a succinct appeal ("walk worthy") it announces the emphasis of chapters 4-6. The inference is that the high calling the Christian has experienced carries with it very weighty responsibilities.

"Walk," a word characteristic of the last half of Ephesians (cf. 4:1,17, 5:2,8,15), is used in the Scriptures to define the course of one's life (cf. 2:2,10). In Genesis, for example, Enoch is said to have "walked with God." And John reminds us of our obligation as Christians to walk even as Jesus walked (1 John 2:6). To "walk worthy of the vocation wherewith ye are called" (vs. 1) means to live in a way that is in harmony with our vocation. The latter word ("vocation") speaks of the calling that belongs to every Christian (cf. 1:18) — to holiness, service, sonship. Beare interprets the term to denote "the place which God has appointed for [Christians] in his plan of the ages" (p. 682).

This appeal for worthy living expresses in a general way the principle that should guide the whole of life. Detailed applications of the principle follow in the remainder of the Epistle, where the apostle describes the various relationships of the Christian — to the community of the redeemed (4:2-16), to society (4:17–5:21), to his family (5:22–6:9), and to the invisible forces of evil (6:10-20).

Verses 2-16, which we must now consider, emphasize the *spiritual* qualities becoming to the life of those who have been called to be God's people. Paul mentions particularly those things essential to right relationships within the community of the redeemed, the things that enhance the fellowship and the overall well-being of the body of Christ. There are three leading ideas:

I. PRACTICE BASIC CHRISTIAN VIRTUES (4:2)

Verse 2 lists five spiritual qualities that characterize the Christian who walks worthily of his calling. The first three — lowliness, meekness, and longsuffering — are kindred ideas. "Lowliness" speaks of humility, the attitude born of a proper estimate of self. Trench understands the root idea to be a recognition of one's "creaturely dependence" on God. Here it is the disposition of persons who are aware of their own smallness and lack of merit before God. "Meekness" conveys the notions of gentleness toward men and submission to God. It is a disposition that manifests itself in mildness, patience, and quiet restraint. Such meekness, of course, is not a natural trait but a work of divine grace in the heart. "Longsuffering," the opposite of short-temperedness, is the disposition of the man who is "slow to anger" (James 1:19). Such a person bears injury and insult without retaliating.

"Forbearance," the fourth quality that attends the worthy Christian life, further explains longsuffering. The man who is "forbearing" is able to make allowances for the faults of his fellow believers, to bear with them in their weaknesses and failings. "In love" shows that this is not to be done grudgingly but in a loving manner, with a sense of "family affection" (Moule, *Epistle to the Ephesians*, p. 104). The Greek word suggests the attitude that seeks the highest good of others.

II. PROMOTE THE UNITY OF THE SPIRIT (4:3-6)

The second essential for living worthily in our relationships within the body of Christ is an earnest effort to promote "the unity of the Spirit."

1. *The Admonition to Unity* (vs. 3). The thought of verses 2,3 should probably be seen as constituting one unit, the admonition reaching its climax in the words, "endeavouring to keep the unity of the Spirit in the bond of peace" (vs. 3). At any rate, this phrase introduces the idea that dominates the passage through verse 6. (We have separated verse 2 from this appeal only to give some prominence to the important words listed in that verse.)

(1) The nature of the unity desired. The context suggests that the

unity Paul had in mind is not external, ecclesiastical union. It is a heart unity and concerns relationships[1] and attitudes rather than organization (cf. Phil. 2:2). Some interpreters look upon the word translated "unity" is an abstract term for what is elsewhere in the Scriptures referred to as "fellowship."

(2) Our responsibility in regard to unity. The production of true unity among God's people is the work of the Spirit. This is why it is called the unity "of [i.e., produced by] the Spirit." It cannot be legislated into being, nor can it be brought about by the mechanics of organization. This does not mean, however, that we are to do nothing to foster and nurture it. Paul expressly charges his readers to endeavor to "keep" the unity of the Spirit. The unity already exists as a spiritual reality; it is our responsibility to keep it intact. The Greek word for "keep," which means first "to watch," then "to keep guard over," suggests vigilant care. For the Greek word translated "endeavouring" there is no precise equivalent in our language. It combines the ideas of haste, eagerness, and zeal. In several passages it is translated "give diligence." (See ASV: 2 Tim. 2:15; 4:21; Heb. 4:11; 2 Peter 1:10). Here it suggests the inward effort that is required in maintaining this unity (cf. NIV, "Make every effort . . .").

2. *The Grounds of Unity* (vss. 4-6) There may be numerous outward things that divide the people of God, but there are fundamental inward experiences that bind them together in an indissoluble spiritual oneness. Verses 4-6 point to seven "ones" that constitute the foundation on which the Spirit effects a true oneness among the redeemed.

These seven unities fall into three groups. The first is "one body . . . one Spirit . . . one hope of your calling" (vs. 4). The "one body" obviously refers to the church, which, as comprised of all God's people, is the body of Christ (cf. 1:23; 2:16). What is said of the church in this broad sense is in the main true of it also in its local manifestations (the churches), but the local concept is not primary here. The church through which "the manifold wisdom of God" is to be made known to "the principalities and powers in heavenly places" (3:10) is seen as one living organism. And just as there is one body, so also there is "one Spirit" who energizes and gives life to that body (cf. 1 Cor. 12:13). Finally, the common goal toward which all who belong to the body are progressing is the "one hope" of sharing ultimately in the glory of God (cf. Rom. 5:2; 1 John 3:2). This hope springs from the calling that God has extended to us (cf. 1:18).

---

[1]Perhaps the primary reference in the word for the first readers of this Epistle was the unity between believing Jews and believing Gentiles, a concept that has received large emphasis in the first three chapters of this Epistle.

Second, there is "one Lord, one faith, one baptism" (vs. 5). The first triad of unities centered in the third Person of the Trinity; this centers in the "one Lord," who is, of course, Jesus Christ. No one can rightly call himself Christian who does not acknowledge Christ in this manner (cf. Rom. 10:9). Early Christians jealously guarded this prerogative of the Savior, and many of them died rather than invoke the Roman emporor as "lord." One of the best-known instances is that of Polycarp, the aged bishop of Smyrna who lived in the second Christian century. When commanded to say, "Caesar is lord," he refused and made the noble confession: "Eighty-six years I have served him, and he has done me no wrong; how then can I blaspheme my Savior and King?" Upon this word the faithful witness was sent to the stake to seal his testimony with his blood.

"Faith" is not to be taken objectively for a system of Christian doctrine. It is not a creed, but the experience of faith or trust in the one Lord.

The "one baptism" is taken by some as a reference to Spirit-baptism, but it seems better to understand it as a reference to water baptism. The point of this verse is that there is one Lord who is to be obeyed and adored; one believing experience that brings people into saving union with that Lord; and one outward, visible ceremony by which believers confess their faith and are openly incorporated into the fellowship of God's people.[2]

This glorious list of spiritual unities is climaxed and crowned by the statement that there is "one God and Father of all" (vs. 6; cf. 1 Cor. 8:6). The one sovereign God is the ultimate source of spiritual unity. There is a sense, of course, in which God as Creator is "Father of all" (cf. Mal. 2:10), but the present context favors the limitation of the concept here to His being Father of all who are Christians. Jewish and Gentile believers, forming one redeemed body, have one God and Father.

This one God is "above all, and through all, and in you all" (vs. 6). (The "all" is general and unqualified, though the primary reference must still be to believers.) The first phrase speaks of God's unshared sovereignty. He has, and can have, no superior. His throne, lifted high over all creation, is paramount and unchallenged. The second phrase speaks of God's immanence, His presence as pervading, controlling, and sustaining all things. Although He is over all, He does not live in remote indifference. His influence and power are everywhere felt. The

---

[2]In speaking of the "one" baptism, Paul seems to have had in mind not the mode (e.g., immersion) but the meaning and significance of the ordinance. "There could as yet be no question of modes of baptism, since these were unknown until later. Deeper than division over modes, which are actually substitutes, is the differing interpretations of the meaning of the ordinance ('sacrament') of baptism. It is out of the departure from the original significance that variation arose in the act of baptism" (Carver, p. 144).

third phrase, "in you all," speaks of God's indwelling and suggests a personal and intimate relationship. The one God and Father dwells "in" His people by His Spirit (cf. 2:22).

III. CONTRIBUTE TO THE GROWTH OF THE CHURCH (4:7-16)

Believers are intended to perform two kinds of ministry. One is a missionary ministry to the world: They are to make disciples of all the nations. The other is an edifying ministry within the body of Christ: Each member is to do his part in the building up of that body until it attains "the measure of the stature of the fulness of Christ." The present passage constitutes a very important discussion of this latter responsibility.

1. *Divine Provision for Growth* (vss. 7-12). God has provided for the growth of His church through the bestowal of manifold gifts on His believing people. These gifts are not to be identified completely with natural endowments; they are to be understood mainly as special capacities for service granted to those who are in Christ (cf. Rom. 12:3-8; 1 Cor. 12:1-31; 1 Peter 4:10,11).[3]

In these verses several matters of considerable importance are taught concerning spiritual gifts:

First, every Christian has a gift of some kind. A gift of "grace" is said to be given "unto every one of us" (vs. 7). Cf. TEV, "Each one of us has been given a special gift." To be sure, not everyone possesses a gift that places him conspicuously before the congregation, but each has a capacity for service somewhere within the body of Christ. And whether others consider it important or not, God deems it so. What a rebuke this truth is to those who imagine that there is nothing they can do in the church!

Second, there is wide diversity in these gifts. Saving grace is the same for all, but each believer's endowment for service is different. This fact is especially pointed up in verse 7. The word *but* marks a change of emphasis. Whereas the emphasis of verses 1-6 has been on the unity of the whole body of Christ, now the thought turns to the diversity of the individual parts that make up the whole. The unity is born of common spiritual experiences. The diversity has to do with the functional services carried out by Christians. The essential truth is that each Christian possesses an individuality that God is pleased to recognize and use in His service.

Third, the special grace (gift) that each Christian has is given "according to the measure of the gift of Christ" (vs. 7). Cf. TEV, "in proportion to what Christ has given"; NIV, "as Christ has apportioned it";

---

[3]The differences in the listings of the gifts suggests that God gave the specific gifts *needed* by the several congregations.

Goodspeed, "in Christ's generous measure." The exalted Lord is sovereign in the distribution of gifts. "The rule is not our merit, nor our previous capacity, nor our asking, but his own good pleasure" (Hodge, p. 212). The logical inference arising from this truth is that each believer should be content with his gift, neither envying those whose gifts are more conspicuous and honorable in the eyes of men, nor looking down on those that seem less so than his own.

Fourth, the bestowal of these gifts is in accordance with a prophetic declaration concerning the ascended Messiah. Alluding to Psalm 68:18, Paul writes, "Wherefore he [God] saith, When he ascended up on high, he led captivity captive, and gave gifts unto men" (vs. 8). The imagery is that of a military conqueror leading captives in triumph and laden with spoils, which he distributes to his followers. In the original context of the psalm it is God who is envisioned as the conqueror, but Paul sees a messianic significance in the words. Thinking of the victory that was achieved at the Cross, he applies the passage to the ascended Christ. Christ, then, is represented as a conqueror enriched by His victories and giving gifts to His people.[4]

Verses 9, 10 are inserted parenthetically to explain verse 8 and to show that the passage quoted refers to Christ. The NEB accurately and clearly brings out the thought: "Now, the word 'ascended' implies that he also descended to the lowest level, down to the very earth. He who descended is no other than he who ascended far above all heavens, so that he might fill the universe." Paul is saying that the ascension of such a divine Person as is described by the psalmist necessarily implies a previous descent by that Person from His heavenly abode. Since Christ is the One who thus descended, it must therefore have been He who was spoken of in the psalm as ascending.

The phrase "lower parts of the earth" (vs. 9) is variously understood. It may for instance, mean parts lower than the earth. Starting from this idea, some interpreters conclude that Christ descended into hell, the place of punishment. But it is seriously doubted that the Scriptures give any warrant to the idea of Christ's going into hell. Nowhere in the Scriptures is it said that Christ saves us by going into hell; consistently the inspired testimony is that He bore our sins in His body on the cross, that by His blood we have forgiveness and redemption.

A variant of this view takes the reference to be to Christ's descent into Hades, that is, the grave or the realm of the dead (cf. Acts 2:25-35, ASV; Rom. 10:7). This interpretation is theologically sound and grammatically legitimate, and many able interpreters subscribe to it.

---

[4]In 1 Corinthians 12 the gifts are represented as given by the Spirit. There is, however, no contradiction, for the Spirit Himself is the Gift of the exalted Christ (Acts 2:33).

Still another way of looking at this phrase, however, is to understand the Greek word for "earth" as a genitive of identity. The meaning, then, is "the parts lower than heaven; that is, the earth." The reference is to the incarnation of Christ (cf. NEB, above). Either of the last two interpretations yields a good meaning, but of these the latter is to be preferred.

In verse 11 we learn that not only does Christ bestow gifts on people; those so gifted are in turn bestowed on the church to serve it in various ways. Some of these "gifts" are enumerated: Some are given to serve as apostles, some as prophets, some as evangelists, and others as pastors and teachers. The point is not that some men received the gift of apostleship, others prophecy, and so on. Rather, the persons thus endowed are themselves the gifts of the ascended Christ to the whole body of Christ. Those who fill the office, no less than the office itself, are gifts to the church.

"Apostles" and "prophets" (cf. 2:20; 3:5) appear to have been confined to the first Christian generation. Apostles, in the stricter use of the word, were those who had seen Christ (1 Cor. 9:1,2), were witnesses of his resurrection (Acts 1:8, 21-23), and were immediately commissioned by Him to preach (Matt. 10:5; Gal. 1:1). In a broader sense, the word was used of those who, though not commissioned directly by Christ as were Paul and the Jerusalem apostles, preached the gospel in close association with such men. Thus, Barnabas is called an apostle (Acts 14:4,14), and Timothy and Silas may be included in the word in 1 Thessalonians 2:6. "Prophets" performed a preaching function; they spoke under the immediate inspiration of the Spirit of God (cf. Acts 11:27ff.; 13:1ff.; 21:4,9; 1 Cor. 14:1ff.). Barclay describes them as "wanderers throughout the church. Their message," he says, "was held to be not the result of thought and study, but the direct result of the Holy Spirit" (p. 172). Smith speaks of them as persons acting and speaking under "extraordinary divine impulse and inspiration, whether in prediction or in teaching" (p. 66). Through them, when there was as yet no New Testament, God gave guidance and direction to His people.

After the writings of the New Testament came into general circulation, the offices of apostle and prophet appear to have been withdrawn;[5] but since evangelists and pastor-teachers are required by every generation, these offices continue. The Greek word for "evangelist" occurs only three times in the New Testament — once of Philip (Acts 21:8), once of Timothy (2 Tim. 4:5), and here. It speaks of one who announces glad

---

[5]Some insist that the term "prophet," in the sense of one proclaiming of God's message, may legitimately be applied to God-called preachers of any age.

tidings, one called and devoted to the direct proclamation of the good news of salvation. We may think of evangelists in New Testament days as missionaries to the unconverted, as itinerant preachers endowed with clear perceptions of saving truth and possessed of unusual power in recommending it to others.

"Pastors and teachers" constitute one office with a dual function. (Observe the wording: "some, pastors and teachers," not "some pastors and some teachers.") The two functions coincide and are combined in one person. As suggested by the terms, a person occupying this office was both to shepherd (which is the idea in the word "pastor") the flock of God and to instruct them in divine truth. We may think of him as performing a settled, rather than itinerant, ministry. This is the only place in the New Testament where "pastor" is used of the office we know by that name. Elsewhere those who fill this office are called "bishops" or "overseers" (Acts 20:28; 1 Tim. 3:2) and "elders" (Acts 20:17; 1 Peter 5:1).

Christ's gift of apostles, prophets, evangelists, and pastor-teachers is for a specific purpose: "for the perfecting of the saints, for the work of the ministry, for the edifying of the body of Christ" (vs. 12). The significance of this verse is obscured by the rendering of KJV. We may translate the thought in this way: "with a view to the equipping [complete outfitting] of the saints for a work of service, [and this] for the building up of the body of Christ." The idea is that the "work of service" is done by the saints. It is the task of apostles, prophets, evangelists, and pastor-teachers to equip them for this service. This meaning fits in well with the statement (vs. 7) that each believer has received a gift of grace, a capacity for service. Apostles, prophets, and all who have been given places of leadership in the church are the means provided for equipping the saints to render this service.

And what is the work of serving to achieve? The answer is in the final phrase of verse 12: "the edifying [building up] of the body of Christ." Toward this end every believer has a contribution to make.

2. *Ultimate Goal of Growth* (vss. 13-16). Verses 13-16 explain what Paul had in mind when he spoke of the building up of the body of Christ — not numerical growth, but the attainment of spiritual maturity on the part of all believers.

(1) The goal defined (vs. 13). A general statement concerning the goal of growth is given in verse 13: "Till we all [the whole number of us] come in [arrive at] the unity of the faith, and of the knowledge of the Son of God, unto a perfect man, unto the measure of the stature of the fulness of Christ." The pivotal words are the conjunction "till," the verb "come," and the prepositions "in" and "unto." The "till" indicates the period during which the ministries mentioned in verse 11 shall last — that is, "till we all come . . . unto the measure of the stature of the fulness

of Christ." This statement does not mean that all the offices mentioned in verse 11 are permanent, for we have already observed that apostles and prophets ceased to be after the first Christian generation. It does mean, however, that the ministries rendered by those offices have abiding significance.

"Come" translates a Greek verb used figuratively here. It means "to arrive," in the sense of reaching a goal.

The goal itself is described by the prepositional phrases that begin: "in . . . unto . . . unto . . . ." First then, the goal of growth is said to be the attainment by the whole body of Christ of "the unity of the faith, and of the knowledge of the Son of God" (ASV). "Unity" is to be taken with both "faith" and "knowledge," and the latter two words are both modified by "of the Son of God." What Paul contemplates is a oneness of faith in, and a oneness of knowledge concerning, the Son of God[6] (cf. Goodspeed). The word "faith" is to be taken in the sense of trust and confidence.[7] The Greek word for "knowledge" is a particularly strong one, denoting full, accurate, and true knowledge.

The goal is further expressed by the words "unto a perfect [full-grown, mature] man." What is meant by attaining "unto" a perfect man is explained by the added phrase, "unto the measure of the stature of the fulness of Christ." That is to say, for the whole company of the redeemed to reach mature manhood in a spiritual sense is for them to attain to the measure of the full stature of Christ, complete conformity to Christ being the ultimate standard of perfection. The idea is not mainly that of individual believers attaining to perfection but rather that of the church, made up of the whole body of believers and viewed as a single organism, reaching its full spiritual stature. "The Church is already the fulness of Christ by the call of God (Eph. 1:23); now she is to attain that fulness in the spiritual growth and life of her members" (Bruce, p. 87).

This goal, in the fullest sense, will not become a reality until the end of time, when the church as the bride of Christ stands before him "glorious," "not having spot, or wrinkle, or any such thing" (Eph. 5:27). However, verses 14-16, which speak of certain qualities that characterize those who have passed beyond the stage of spiritual childhood, appear to contemplate at least a relative fulfillment in time.

(2) *The Marks of Maturity* (vss. 14-16). Verse 13 has given a general statement of the goal of growth set before God's people; verses 14-16 now set forth the results of attaining that goal. We may think of these as the marks of spiritual maturity.

---

[6]The TCNT suggests a different idea: "Unity which is given by faith and by a fuller knowledge of the Son of God."

[7]The NIV, however, follows KJV and translates the word in its objective sense: "unity in *the* faith and in the knowledge of the Son of God" (italics mine).

One prominent trait of the mature Christian is doctrinal stability (vs. 14). When we arrive at the measure of the full stature of Christ we are no longer infants at the mercy of error. Paul put it like this: ". . . no longer children, tossed to and fro [like waves of the sea], and carried about with [by] every wind of doctrine" (asv). "Children" is in contrast with the "perfect man" of verse 13. "Tossed to and fro, and carried about" are words that might be used of a ship abandoned on a storm-tossed sea — a graphic figure of instability and helplessness. "Wind of doctrine" suggests the shifting currents of false teaching, blowing now from this quarter, now from that. To be "carried about by every wind of doctrine" is to be swept along by whatever religious currents may be blowing most strongly at the time.

The particular "wind of doctrine" Paul had in mind for his time was the incipient gnosticism threatening the churches of Asia when he wrote this letter. Combining a bare minimum of Christian truth with Jewish ritualism and Oriental mysticism, this heresy perverted the doctrine of salvation by grace, misconstrued the character of the Christian life, and cast a shadow over the glory and majesty of Jesus Christ. Against this system of error Paul warned the Colossians: "Beware lest any man spoil you through philosophy and vain deceit, after the tradition of men, after the rudiments of the world, and not after Christ" (2:8).

Persons who lack spiritual stability, whether they live in the first or the twentieth century, are always easy prey for peddlers of religious fads and heresies. They have, as Eadie says, "just enough Christian intelligence to unsettle them, and make them the prey of every idle suggestion, the sport of every religious novelty" (p. 316).

False teaching wields its peculiar power "by the sleight of men, and by cunning craftiness." Cf. rsv; "by the cunning of men, by their craftiness and deceitful wiles." The word translated "sleight" (rsv, "cunning") originally meant "dice-throwing." It came to be a term for clever trickery and deception, which is its meaning here. (Beare, however, understands the phrase to mean "the fickleness of men.") "Cunning" (rsv, "craftiness") translates a word that betokens a readiness to do anything. It describes people who will stop at nothing in their effort to ensnare gullible and fickle souls. "Craftiness" is "deceitful scheming" (niv). The whole idea of "cunning craftiness" (kjv) is taken by Goodspeed to mean "ingenuity in inventing error." What a vivid description of the malicious ways of those not anchored to the truth!

A second characteristic of the mature Christian is love (vs. 15). Verse 14 has shown that to arrive at mature spiritual manhood means to be no longer infants at the mercy of error. Verse 15 puts the same thought in terms of adherence to truth and growing up to Christ. "Speaking the truth" translates a single Greek word that has been interpreted in many ways: holding truth, maintaining truth, living the truth, or speaking truth. It may be that we should understand the word as including all of these meanings. At any rate, the emphasis falls on the words "in love." Even truth can be held and dispensed in a deceitful spirit; and even if deceit is not present, mere doctrinal orthodoxy can be a very cold and lifeless thing. Paul's thought was that sound teaching should be held, handled, and lived in a loving spirit. In so doing we shall fully grow up to Christ. Goodspeed translates, "We must lovingly hold to the truth and grow up into perfect union with him who is the head — Christ himself."

A final trait of the mature Christian is that he faithfully fulfills his appointed function within the body of Christ and thus contributes his part to the overall growth of that body (vs. 16). The language of the verse is very compact and highly figurative. It pictures the body of Christ (the church) as an "organism in which each member contributes to the growth of the whole by receiving and passing on the life drawn from Christ, the Head" (Hunter, pp. 66,67). In this way the life and strength of the head flow into the body, permeating its every part. The main statement is this: "From whom the whole body . . . maketh increase [growth] of the body unto the edifying of itself in love (cf. RSV, "from whom the whole body . . . makes bodily growth and upbuilds itself in love.") Drawing from Christ, the body effects its own growth. And this process takes place "according to the effectual working in the measure of every part." That is to say, the growth of the body of Christ is on the scale of, i.e., in proportion to, the "working" or the proper functioning of each individual Christian (cf. vs. 12). The thought is that each Christian is a point of supply for the body of Christ, a channel to receive and pass on life from Christ. The TEV expresses the entire thought clearly: "Under his [Christ's] control all the different parts of the body fit together, and the whole body is held together by every joint with which it is provided. So when each separate part works as it should, the whole body grows and builds itself up through love."

> To know, to do, the Head's commands,
> For this the body lives and grows;
> All speed of feet and skill of hands
> Is for Him spent, and from Him flows.

> — Author unknown

FOR FURTHER STUDY

1. Read Ephesians and mark each occurrence of the words *walk*, *calling*, (or *vocation*), *call*, etc.

2. Compare the list of Christ's gifts to the church given in Ephe-

sians 4 with the lists of gifts in Romans 12 and 1 Corinthians 12. Write down the similarities and the differences.

3. Study the word *Hades* in a Bible dictionary.

4. Spurgeon has a sermon on "The Ascension of Christ" in his *Treasury of the Bible: New Testament*.

CHAPTER 9

The Daily Walk of God's New People: Moral Obligations

(Ephesians 4:17–5:21)

The Ephesian letter pulsates with a double desire: that believers may have a fuller comprehension of what God in Christ is doing in and for them, and that their lives may in some measure correspond to His work of grace. In 4:1-16 Paul has dwelt on those responsibilities that pertain especially to our relationships within the body of Christ. At verse 17 he turns to discuss duties, mostly of a moral nature, that concern our relation not only to fellow believers but more especially to the world about us. These are described first by a general statement (4:17-24) and then (4:25–5:21) in more detail.

I. A Clean Break With Old Pagan Ways (4:17-24)

The use of the words *therefore* and *walk* (vs. 17) points us back to the same words in 4:1. *Testify*, a strong word of solemn appeal, means "to insist" or "implore." The phrase "in the Lord" suggests that Paul is conscious of such a connection with the Lord that he speaks in the Lord's name and feels that his words are clothed with divine authority. The appeal itself is stated both negatively and positively. The negative part concerns the "walk" of the Gentiles (vss. 17-19); the positive part revolves around the concept of "truth [as it] is in Jesus" (vss. 20-24).

1. *The Walk of the Gentiles* (vss. 17-19). Paul insists that his readers must "no longer walk as the Gentiles . . . walk" (vs. 17, ASV). The KJV has "other Gentiles," but the best manuscripts omit "other." This reading suggests that Paul's readers were no longer to be regarded as Gentiles (i.e., pagans). They were now "fellow-citizens with the saints" and a part of "the household of God" (2:19). "No longer" implies that once they lived as the Gentiles (i.e., in a typically pagan way). Now, however, they must renounce the life and wicked ways of their pagan neighbors and see to it that their daily walk conforms to their new relationship.

The apostle proceeds to enumerate some of the salient features of pagan life in the first century: vanity, darkness, alienation, ignorance,

99

hardness, loss of feeling, lasciviousness, uncleanness, greediness. It is a grim and revolting picture that he draws, in many respects parallel to the statement of Romans 1:18ff.

First, Paul speaks of "the vanity of their mind" (vs. 17) and their being "darkened" in "the understanding" (vs. 18). "Vanity," a word often associated with idol worship, suggests emptiness, futility, and purposelessness — life with no real meaning, no goal. The thought is not that unregenerate minds are empty. It is that they are filled with things that lead to nothing. Cf. NEB, "good-for-nothing notions." To have "the understanding darkened" is to be without the faculty of discernment, to be unable to distinguish between right and wrong.

Next, non-Christians are described as "being alienated from the life of God" (vs. 18). That is to say, they are separated from the life that comes from God, held in the grip of spiritual death (cf. 2:1). The cause of this estrangement is twofold: "the ignorance that is in them" (vs. 18) and "the blindness of their heart" (vs. 18). Instead of "blindness" most modern versions have "hardness." The Greek word originally meant "petrifaction" but came eventually to be used by medical writers of numbness, insensibility, callousness. Here it betokens an insensitivity to spiritual things. Beare sees it as a "steeling of the will against every good impulse" (p. 696).

"Being past feeling" (vs. 19) continues the idea suggested by "hardness." The word primarily means "to cease to feel pain," then "to cease to care" — whether through despair or through recklessness. In this passage it describes reckless abandon, a state of moral insensibility wherein one no longer feels the reproaches of conscience. The TEV has "they have lost all feeling of shame."

Being thus destitute of compunctions, pagan people gave "themselves over unto lasciviousness, to work all [every kind of] uncleanness with greediness" (vs. 19). Three frightful words are used in this statement. The first is "lasciviousness," the Greek word denoting lewd or wanton conduct that shocks public decency. The one who can be so described no longer cares to hide his sin; it does not matter to him who sees his shame, so long as he can gratify his desires. The second main word ("uncleanness") is indicative here of moral uncleanness (TEV uses "indecency"). The word translated "greediness" is built on a root that means "to have more." It describes a disposition that has absolutely no regard for the rights of others. Very wide in scope, it is used sometimes in reference to material things (translated "covetousness") and sometimes of such things as sexual indulgence (translated "greediness"), as here. "It is the spirit of the man," explains Barclay, "who does not care whom he hurts and what method he uses so long as he gets what he desires" (p. 182).

Commenting on this description of ancient pagan life, one writer asks whether Paul "put too much lampblack into his painting." He goes on to say:

> Let us answer this question with another one: If Paul were writing today, would his picture of those who live the pagan life be much rosier? Some cultured humanists of our day who repudiate the Christian faith undoubtedly lead morally respectable lives; but not all. A goodly number of them dislike Christianity not so much for intellectual as for moral reasons, namely, because it insists on purity and chastity. In any case, no clear-sighted observer of our human situation can deny that when men and women reject the blessings and sanctions of Christianity, they relapse into ways of living not unlike Paul's Gentiles. Who will dare to say that "the world" today (which is the equivalent of "the Gentiles" in our letter) is not full of drunkenness, gambling, sexual vice, and that ruthless self-assertion which cares nothing for its neighbor's rights? (Hunter, p. 67).

2. *The Truth As It Is in Jesus* (vss. 20-24). Over against the walk of the Gentiles the apostle places the "truth as it is in Jesus." The "ye" (vs. 20) is in sharp contrast to "Gentiles" (vs. 17). The force of the Greek may be brought out by translating, "But *you* — you did not thus learn the Christ." The readers of this letter did indeed learn the Christ, but not in such a way as to condone their old pagan habits. When they received the gospel, they were taught that Christian discipleship required the renunciation of all pagan vices and the cultivation of true Christian holiness.

The readers had been taught "truth as it is in Jesus" (vs. 21). No article is used with "truth" in the Greek, the thought being that whatever is truth or spiritual reality is embodied in Christ. Such truth can be known only by those who have "learned Christ," have "heard him," and have been "taught by him" (vss. 20,21).

The essence of truth as it is in Jesus is defined in the Greek by three infinitive constructions. In the English text these are expressed by the verbal constructions "put off" (vs. 22), "be renewed" (vs. 23), and "put on" (vs. 24).[1]

(1) Putting off the old man (vs. 22). A part of truth as it is in Jesus is that "ye [did] put off [once for all] concerning the former conversation [manner of life] the old man" (vs. 22). The "old man" (RSV, "old nature"; NIV, "old self") is an important phrase. Romans 6:6 affirms that "our old man is crucified with" Christ. Colossians 3:9 asserts, "Ye have put off the old man with his doings" (ASV). The term personifies the moral and spiritual state of the pre-Christian life (cf. Gal. 2:20). Moule understands it to mean "all that I was as an unregenerate son of Adam, liable to eternal doom, and the slave of sin" (*Cambridge Bible*, p. 118).

---

[1] The RSV gives these infinitives imperative force. We are construing them as explanatory.

The "old man" is not renewed, is not converted. He is under sentence of death and is in process of decaying. He grows more and more "corrupt" by virtue of the deceitful lusts that belong to his nature (vs. 22). The only remedy is to renounce him completely, nail him to the cross, and replace him with the "new man" (vs. 24). When Paul speaks of "putting off" the old man, the figure is that of stripping off a garment. The tense points to a definite, decisive, and permanent act.

(2) Being renewed in the spirit of the mind (vs. 23). Truth as it is in Jesus teaches that believers are being continually "renewed in the spirit [disposition] of" the "mind" (vs. 23). This renovation should be compared with "the vanity" of mind that marked the Gentiles (vs. 17). The word for "be renewed" is in the present tense, denoting something continuous and progressive in the life of the believer. It represents an experience that is the antithesis of the growing corruptness of the old man (Cf. 2 Corinthians 4:16).

(3) Putting on the new man (vs. 24). Finally, truth as it is in Jesus means "that ye [did] put on [once for all] the new man" (vs. 24). This statement is the positive counterpart of the negative in verse 22. The old man was stripped off; the new man was "put on." The two acts are absolutely inseparable.

The "new man" is the new nature, the new self. This new self, Paul teaches, has been created "after [the likeness of] God" and manifests itself "in righteousness and holiness of truth" (vs. 24, ASV; cf. Col. 3:10). "After [the likeness of] God" perhaps suggests the immortality of the new life, in contrast with the growing decay of the old nature. "Righteousness" in this context likely refers to our manward behavior, right dealing between person and person. "Holiness," on the other hand has to do with our conduct toward God. It includes here the ideas of consecration and devotion. Both righteousness and holiness are the proper fruit of embracing the truth as it is in Jesus.

II. The Virtues That Become the New Man (4:25-32)

The "wherefore" (vs. 25) shows that the detailed instructions that follow are rooted in, and grow out of, the principles set forth in 4:20-24. Christians, in principle, put off the old man and put on the new at conversion. But what is true already in principle must be made real in actual practice. The new nature imparted at conversion must be cultivated; the old must be subdued.

In verses 25-32 five classes of sins, viewed as the rags that belonged to the old man, are mentioned; the corresponding virtues, viewed as the robes that should adorn the new man, are set in striking contrast.

First, "lying" must be banished from the Christian's life, and in its place "truth" must be cultivated (vs. 25). "Lying" — the word includes every kind of deception — is one of the chief characteristics of the old man. It is preeminently a heathen vice, as missionaries to pagan lands abundantly testify. Unfortunately, it is not confined to pagan lands. People in a so-called Christian culture need also to be admonished at this point. We see on every hand dishonesty in personal relations, unscrupulous practices in business, and corruption and deception in government.

Instead of lying, the Christian is to "speak the truth with his neighbor" (vs. 25b, RSV). The motive in doing so is found in our mutual relationships within the body of Christ: "We are the members one of another" (vs. 25c). Cf. TEV, "we are all members together in the body of Christ"; TCNT, "we are united to one another like the parts of a body." See Colossians 3:9 for another motive for truthfulness.·

Second, sinful anger must be controlled and subdued (vss. 26,27). There is a place for anger of a certain sort ("righteous indignation") in the Christian life (cf. Mark 3:5), and verse 26 leaves room for this. The Greek verb is perhaps a permissive imperative: not, "Be angry," but, "You may be angry."[2] The NEB renders it, "If you are angry"; NIV, "In your anger." But this permission concerning anger is strongly qualified by two additional statements. (1) It must be carefully guarded so as not to pass into sin (vs. 26a). Anger that is selfish, undisciplined, and uncontrolled is always sinful; and even that which starts out as righteous indignation all too easily degenerates to this level. (2) Anger must never be cherished: "Let not the sun go down upon your wrath" (vs. 26b). That is to say, anger must not be carried over from one day into the next. Anger that is not speedily deposed soon takes deep root in the heart. When this happens, the devil — "slanderer" is the meaning of the Greek word — gains "room to act," a foothold from which to exploit us (vs. 27).

A third vice that has no place in the Christian life is stealing (vs. 28). Paul had in mind the person who was a thief before his conversion and who may have been in danger of falling back into his old ways. Instead of this, he is encouraged to engage in honest toil so that he not only meets his own needs but may have something to share with those less fortunate than himself.

"Corrupt communication" (vs. 29), the fourth vice to be named, may be understood as either foul-mouthed talk or worthless speech. Such language had likely been habitual with many of Paul's readers before their conversion. It is unbecoming for a Christian and must be completely renounced. The suppression of bad language, however, is not enough. Conscious effort is to be made to use language that will edify

---

[2]Some interpreters think justifiable anger is not at all involved in this passage. The author's one point, says Beare, "is that we must expell it from our hearts before the day is out" (p. 700).

and "minister grace [benefit] unto the hearers" (vs. 29).

Verse 30 is to be taken in the closest possible connection with what has been said in the preceding verses. The point is that lying, resentment, stealing, and especially the use of filthy, unedifying language by Christians grieve (Goodspeed, "offend") the indwelling Spirit. This fact explains the misery of many believers, for it is precisely by reason of permitting such practices that they have lost the joy, peace, and blessedness that they once knew. Cowper referred to such an experience when he wrote:

> Where is the blessedness I knew
>   When first I saw the Lord?
> Where is the soul-refreshing view
>   Of Jesus and His Word?
>
> What peaceful hours I once enjoyed!
>   How sweet their mem'ry still!
> But they have left an aching void
>   The world can never fill.
>
> Return, O Holy Dove, return,
>   Sweet messenger of rest;
> I hate the sins that made Thee mourn,
>   And drove Thee from my breast.

The Spirit, Paul explains, has "sealed" us "unto the day of redemption" (vs. 30b; cf. 1:13). The thought is that he has marked us as His own with a view to the day of full redemption. Compare TEV, "the Spirit is God's mark of ownership on you, a guarantee that the day will come when God will set you free."

The final class of sins, listed in verse 31, all have to do with bad temper. "Bitterness" describes the sour, resentful spirit of a person who broods over the injuries and slights he receives and refuses to be reconciled. "Wrath" is literally a sudden outburst of passion; Goodspeed translates it "rage." "Anger" is a settled feeling. Such eruptions of temper show themselves both in "clamour" and in "evil speaking." The first of these words likely refers to public quarreling (TCNT, "brawling"; NEB, "angry shouting"); the latter word may be taken in this context to mean slanderous whispers (cf. Knox, "insulting talk), though TCNT translates it "abusive language" (cf. NEB, "cursing"). These things, together "with all malice," are to be decisively "put away." The Greek word for "malice" may be defined as "a vicious disposition" or "spite." Moule understands it as "the deep unkindness of the self-centered, Christless heart" (*Ephesian Studies*, p. 235). Certainly, it should have no place in a believer's life.

The vacuum created when these vices are ejected from the heart is to be filled by the lovely virtues of kindness, tenderheartedness, forgiveness, and love (vs. 32). "Be ye kind" might be more literally rendered "become kind," suggesting that we are not kind by nature. Weymouth translates it, "learn to be kind." The Greek word for "kind" is built on a root that means "useful" or "helpful." The NEB has "generous." To be "tenderhearted" is to have a compassionate feeling toward the weaknesses and miseries of others. "Forgiving" is the rendering of a word of unusually rich content. Being built on the same root as the word for "grace," it first means "to give freely," then "to pardon" or "forgive." The supreme example as well as the sacred incentive for this attitude is that which God has done for us — as Paul puts it, "even as God for Christ's sake [literally, 'in Christ,' i.e., acting in Christ] hath forgiven you" (vs. 32b).

III. IMITATORS OF GOD (5:1-14)

The appeal to "be . . . followers of God, as dear children" is the main thought of 5:1-14. "Followers" (imitators) translates *mimetai*, from which we get "mimic." The TEV paraphrases, "try to be like" God. Goodspeed has "follow God's example."

"As dear children" indicates that we are to imitate God because we are His children. Such imitation, then, is not the means of our acceptance with God but the result of it.

The passage speaks of two special areas in which we must imitate God: love (vss. 1,2) and light (purity) (vss. 3-14).

1. *In Love* (vss. 1,2). Paul's word is "Walk in love, as Christ also hath loved us" (vs. 2). "Walk" (cv. 4:1) is a present tense, denoting action that is habitual. To walk habitually "in love" is to make that virtue the ruling principle of our life.

There are two distinguishing marks of this love. The first, forgiveness, is an inference (note "therefore") drawn from the closing verse of chapter 4. God in Christ has forgiven you (4:32); you then, as His beloved children, are to be imitators of Him and cherish a forgiving spirit toward one another (5:1).

A second mark of this love is sacrifice: "As Christ also hath loved us, and hath given himself for us" (vs. 2). John wrote, "By this we know love, that he laid down his life for us; and we ought to lay down our lives for the brethren" (1 John 3:16, RSV). Such love is not mere sentiment and feeling. It gives all, counting no sacrifice too great for the object on which it is fixed.

2. *In Purity* (vss. 3-14). Regulated as it was by the will of God, Christ's was a holy love that could never tolerate evil and had in it no admixture of impurity. This thought leads Paul into a discussion of moral purity as an imperative Christian duty. It may be that the readers were being subjected to the teachings of those who defended immorality on

the ground that the deeds of the body do not defile the soul. (This was the heresy combated in Colossians and in 1 John.) Paul, in his discussion, mentions sins to be avoided (vss. 3,4), and the reasons for avoiding them (vss. 7-14).

(1) Sins to be avoided (vss. 3,4). The sins to be especially avoided are listed in two groups, each containing three related vices. Mention is made of "fornication, and all uncleanness, or covetousness." These iniquitous vices are to be so far removed from Paul's readers that they are not even to be "named among" them (vs. 3). Paul means that these sins are to be so foreign to Christians that not the slightest intimation or suspicion of their presence among them can occur. There may be the added notion that there is not even room for discussion as to whether those sins are permissible for Christians.

The Greek word for "fornication" originally denoted the practice of consorting with prostitutes, but it came to signify any form of sexual evil. Several versions render it "immorality." The Gentile world of Paul's day regarded this sin as a matter of moral indifference, and it was indulged in without scruple by all classes of people. Infidelity in marriage was frightfully common, and homosexuality had for centuries been an accepted way of life. Some of the great pagan temples were staffed by hundreds of priestesses who were nothing more than religious prostitutes placed there for the use of the men who came to offer their licentious worship to heathen deities.

"All uncleanness" and "covetousness" go together, the "or" that joins them indicating that though they are different sins, they belong to the same class. "Uncleanness" is nearly always used in the New Testament in a moral sense. Here TEV translates it "indecency." "All uncleanness" is to be understood in the sense of every kind of sexual uncleanness or indecency. "Covetousness," which is considered very lightly by many people today, is unsparingly condemned in the New Testament and is several times classed by Paul with the grossest kinds of immorality. So diluted has our thinking become that one sometimes hears it said of a person, "He is a good Christian. His only fault is covetousness." In light of the present passage it might be just as proper to describe a woman as both a virtuous lady and an infamous prostitute. It is possible that the Greek word should be interpreted here as meaning sensual self-indulgence — the attitude that seeks gratification of self regardless of the cost to others. See the discussion of 4:19, where the same word is translated "greediness." In the present passage NEB has "ruthless greed."

Verse 4 lists three other kindred sins: "Neither filthiness, nor foolish talking, nor jesting" are to be named among believers. The word translated "filthiness" appears here to refer to indecent, shameful speech — possibly to filthy stories (cf. NEB, *Living Bible*). The TCNT, however, interprets it to mean "shameful conduct"; NIV, "obscenity."

"Foolish talking" (RSV, "silly talk") includes not only coarse vulgarity but all idle gossip as well. The Greek word means "fool-talk" and suggests that those who jest of unclean things and in general engage in debasing conversation demonstrate that they are fools. "Jesting" (RSV, "levity"; NEB, "flippant talk") should be understood as denoting buffoonery and ribaldry. Paul is not condemning lively and sanctified humor. He is not calling upon us to be long-faced, gloomy people who dare not tell anything that evokes innocent laughter. A good, hearty laugh is often medicine for the soul. But there are some things of which Christians should never make jokes — some are too sacred, some too filthy.

In the words "which are not convenient" (vs. 4), Paul gathers up filthiness, foolish talking, and jesting, and describes them as things not seemly for believers. True Christian cheerfulness and buoyancy of spirit should manifest themselves "rather" in "giving of thanks" (vs. 4). Remembrance of the goodness of God, writes Beare, is "an impenetrable barrier to filthiness of every kind" (p. 707). This giving of thanks is a recurring theme in the companion Epistle to the Colossians.

(2) Reasons for avoiding sins of uncleanness (vss. 5,6). Paul has used stern words about sins of uncleanness. Their utter incongruity with Christian profession is now brought out by two further considerations: the character of God's kindgom and the fact of God's wrath.

The character of God's kingdom is such that "no whoremonger, nor unclean person, nor covetous man . . . hath any inheritance" in it (vs. 5).[3] Those who are so described show a character wholly incompatible with that divine kingdom into which only the regenerate may enter (John 3:3). Their lives bear witness to the fact that they are strangers to grace and are still held in "the gall of bitterness, and in the bond of iniquity" (cf. Acts 8:23).

The "whoremonger" (literally, "fornicator") is one who practices any kind of sexual immorality. The "unclean person," in this context, is the person whose life is marked by sexual impurity. It is thought by many that the "covetous man" is "an idolater" because in his greed for things — whether material or sensual — he sets up in his heart an object of worship other than God. Weymouth, however, brings out a different idea in his version: "For be well assured that no fornicator or immoral person and no profligate — or in other words idol-worshipper — has any share. . . ." This reference reflects that idolatry and sensuality were inextricably bound together. It is possible that the equation of the

---

[3]The opening words of this verse, weakly rendered in KJV by "for this ye know," should be read in a modern translation. The NEB has "For be very sure of this."

covetous person with an idolator is rooted in those Old Testament Scriptures that speak of Israel's worship of idols as spiritual adultery (cf. Hos. 2:5; Ezek. 23:37, et al.).

The "kingdom of Christ and of God" is the redemptive rule of God that delivers people from the powers of evil and brings to them "righteousness, and peace, and joy in the Holy Ghost" (Rom. 14:17). The church, which is not to be identified with the kingdom, is the fellowship of those who have accepted Christ's offer of the kingdom and have submitted to its rule. In a sense, the kingdom creates the church and the church is the instrument for extending the kingdom. It is here called "the kingdom of Christ" because God has committed the administration of it to Christ's hands (Luke 22:29). In a sense, the redemptive rule of God is embodied in Him. In His person and mission that rule has already invaded human history (Matt. 3:2; 12:28) and is now moving toward a glorious consummation when Christ, having put all His enemies under His feet, will return the kingdom to the Father (1 Cor. 15:24-28).

A second reason for avoiding sins of uncleanness is the fact of God's wrath (vs. 6). Apparently there were not wanting in Paul's day (as there surely are not in our day) those who by specious arguments would excuse and condone the sins under discussion. Paul may have had in mind those who were influenced by gnosticism to believe that sins of the body could not affect the soul and therefore had no bearing on the spiritual life. Or, he may allude to those who felt that freedom from law meant license to sin (cf. Gal. 5:1ff.).

The readers are warned against letting anyone, whoever he may be, lead them astray by "vain [empty] words." Such words are void of all truth and reality and if heeded can only lead to spiritual tragedy. It is because of these very sins that "the wrath of God" comes "upon the children of disobedience" (cf. 2:2,3). The tense of the verb "cometh" is present and strongly suggests the certainty of the divine visitation on the workers of iniquity.

In verse 7 Paul's readers are urgently enjoined not to become partners in sin with those on whom the wrath of God must inevitably fall. If they recoil from contemplation of partnership in their punishment, let them also recoil in horror from partnership in their sins. In a general way this idea is developed through verse 14.

Once the readers were darkness, but now they have become "light in the Lord" (vs. 8). In their unconverted state, ignorance and sin had so penetrated their being that they were not merely *in* the dark; they were the very *embodiment* of darkness. Conversely, in their converted state the light of the gospel has so penetrated them that they are themselves light. In them the light has become visible and is the dominant trait of their character. The meaning of the verse is brought out in its contrasts — "sometimes" (better, "once") and "now"; "darkness" and "light." The emphasis, however, rests on "were," which in the Greek is the first word of its clause. To say that the readers "were" darkness is to imply that deeds of darkness are now behind them. Such things are no longer in harmony with their character, and they must not revert to them.

Three responsibilities are rooted in this concept of believers being "light in the Lord." First, they are to "walk as children of light" (vs. 8). Their conduct must conform to that which is most essential in their character.

Second, those who are light in the Lord are to produce the fruit of the light (see ASV, RSV). This fruit is defined as "goodness and righteousness and truth" (vs. 9, ASV). These may be called the cardinal qualities that mark life in the light. The Greek word translated by "goodness" stresses kindliness and benevolence, the spirit that makes one want to help others. "Righteousness" is regard for the rights of others, giving both to men and to God that which is their due. "Truth" concerns not only what is spoken; it is truth of idea as well, that is, sincerity, straightforwardness.

The third responsibility of the children of light is to reprove "the unfruitful works of darkness" (vs. 11). Such works are "unfruitful" because they produce no goodness, give no satisfaction and joy (cf. vs. 9). To "reprove" (vs. 11) the works of darkness is to expose them, to turn the light on them and show that they are unfruitful and belong to the darkness. It is not enough merely to withdraw, to "have no fellowship with" them. The light of believers must blaze out into the darkness and be a constant condemnation of the darkness.

Verse 12 tells why it is imperative to reprove the works of darkness: They are so unspeakably bad, especially those done secretly, that the Christian has no other recourse.

Verse 13, a very difficult verse that is variously translated, offers still another reason for reproving the deeds of darkness. The idea seems to be: Your responsibility is to reprove these things, for you are light, and light is that which makes manifest. Others think the underlying thought is that darkness cannot exist in the presence of light. Once light is let in on evil (the darkness), the evil is not only seen for what it is but is transformed. Beare, an advocate of this view, writes, "The power of the light not only reveals, but penetrates and transforms into its own likeness whatever it illuminates" (p. 711).

Verse 14, which is introduced as a quotation, is understood by many interpreters to express the substance of Isaiah 60:1. By others it is thought to be a quotation from an early baptismal hymn — perhaps sung at the moment the convert was raised from the water. Either way, it may be taken as an example of the way in which reproof is to be administered. That is, the reproof of sinners is to take the form of an urgent call to them to let the light of Christ shine on them. Its aim is never to be mere rebuke; it seeks the conversion of the sinner.

IV. WALKING CIRCUMSPECTLY (5:15-21).

This portion of the Ephesian letter constitutes an exhortation to the readers to live like wise men. "See then that ye walk circumspectly, not as fools, but as wise" (vs. 15). The word "circumspectly" suggests looking all around, giving attention to all circumstances and consequences as one might do when passing through a very dangerous place. The Greek word, however, expresses the idea of living in strict conformity to a standard, guarding against anything that would be improper or unbecoming for the Christian. It may be translated, "Watch carefully, then, how you walk." The TEV has "So pay close attention to how you live." The thought is further explained by the words "not as fools, but as wise." Believers are to walk as people having the character of wise men, not fools.

Verses 16-21 define the walk of wisdom in three particulars.

1. *Redeeming the Time* (vs. 16). First, to walk wisely means that one will make the most of every opportunity — "redeeming the time" (vs. 16). The Greek word for "redeeming" is a market term meaning "to buy out" or "purchase completely." "Time" is the translation of a Greek word that came to mean something rather like "opportunity." To "buy out the opportunity" is to make the most of one's time, to pay the price in effort and exertion that is necessary in using it. TEV has "make good use of every opportunity."

The Greeks represented the concept of opportunity in sculpture by a youth with wings on his feet and back, having long hair in front and being bald in back. The suggestion was that if opportunity is grasped at all it must be grasped by the forelock. The application for us is clear: Opportunities for Christian service are brief seasons that soon slip by. The wise Christian will recognize them and use them while he can.

A reason for redeeming the time is given in the words "because the days are evil" (vs. 16b). The reference is to conditions unfavorable to the Christian. These must never be taken as an excuse for relaxation but as an incentive for greater earnestness.

2. *Understanding the Will of God* (vs. 17). The primary consideration for the Christian must never be what is most profitable financially, what is most pleasurable or enjoyable, or what will bring the greatest personal advantage or honor. His first concern is to discern what God wills him to be and to do. This course is the way of wisdom, and anything

short of it betrays a mind lacking in moral intelligence.

3. *Being Filled With the Spirit* (vss. 18-21). Verse 18 contains both a negative and a positive command: "Be not drunk with wine, wherein is excess; but be filled with the Spirit."[4] Drunkenness is alluded to as a concrete example of the heedless folly referred to in verse 17. It is forbidden because it leads to "excess," "dissipation," or "ruin." John Eadie's words, written long ago, are still all too true. Speaking of intemperance, he declared that there is in it

> that kind of dissoluteness which brooks no restraint, which defies all efforts to reform it, and which sinks lower and lower into hopeless and helpless ruin. . . . This tremendous sin . . . is all the more to be shunned as its hold is so great on its victims, for with periodical remorse there is periodical inebriety; the fatal cup is again coveted and drained; while character, fortune, and life are risked and lost in the gratification of an appetite of all others the most brutal in form and brutifying in result. There are few vices out of which there is less hope of recovery — its haunts are so numerous and its hold is so tremendous (p. 397).

The emphasis of the verse, however, falls on the positive command, "Be filled with the Spirit." The Greek text, which may read, "Be filled in spirit," suggests to some interpreters that spirit (as opposed to the physical part of our being) is the sphere in which we are to be filled. It is much better, however, to understand the reference to be to the Holy Spirit. Viewed in this manner, the injunction may be translated, "Be filled through [or by] the Spirit." But it seems preferable to follow the rendering of KJV, ASV, RSV, NASB, and others ("be filled with the Spirit") or that of NEB ("let the Holy Spirit fill you"). Robinson feels that the language combines the ideas of a "fulness which comes through the Spirit" and a "fulness which consists in being full of the Spirit" (p. 204). To be full of the Spirit is to possess as much of the Spirit as one can contain. Perhaps there is the added notion of being permeated by His presence and power, being brought under his gracious control.

Anyone desiring to grasp the meaning of this passage should study the writings of Luke, for whom the idea of a "filling" was a favorite (cf. Luke 1:15; 41,67; 4:1; Acts 2:4; 4:8,31; 6:3,5; 7:55; 9:17; 11:24; 13:9,52).

In the present passage the subject of the verb is plural, indicating that the experience should not be looked upon as exceptional, nor as the prerogative of only a select few. The tense of the verb is present,

---

[4]It is instructive to compare some of the different renderings of this verse: TEV, "Do not get drunk with wine, which will only ruin you; instead, be filled with the Spirit." TCNT, "Do not drink wine to excess, for that leads to profligacy; but seek to be filled with the Spirit of God." NEB, "Do not give way to drunkenness and the dissipation that goes with it, but let the Holy Spirit fill you." Knox, "Do not besot yourselves with wine; that leads to ruin. Let your contentment be in the Holy Spirit." Weymouth, "Do not indulge in much wine — a thing in which excess is so easy — but drink deeply of God's Spirit."

pointing up either an action that is to be repeated from time to time or an action that is continuous. In this respect, the "filling" is different from the baptism in/with/by the Spirit. The latter is experienced by all believers and is never repeated (cf. 1 Cor. 12:13). Moreover, the New Testament contains not a single command to be baptized in/with/by the Spirit. The voice of the verb is passive, indicating that we are acted upon by the Spirit (cf. NEB).

Carnal intoxication leads to ruin,[5] but the fullness wrought by the Spirit of God issues in joyfulness (vs. 19), thankfulness (vs. 20), and mutual submission (vs. 21). These are the qualities that mark the Spirit-filled life.

(1) Joyfulness. "Speaking to yourselves in psalms and hymns and spiritual songs" is a general expression of glad and cheerful discourse, defined more precisely by the phrase "singing and making melody in [with] your heart to the Lord" (vs. 19). Those who are filled with the Spirit express among themselves their joyous emotions in psalms, hymns, and spiritual songs. The reference may be both to social conversation and to meetings of divine worship. Both are to be marked by hallowed and joyful praise.

Too sharp a distinction between "psalms," "hymns," and "songs" should not be drawn. The language is intended to emphasize rich variety of sacred song, not to give instruction in ancient hymnology. If any differentiation is made, "psalms" may be taken to refer to Old Testament psalms, while "hymns" and "spiritual songs" both refer to distinctively Christian compositions, the latter possibly being impromptu rhythmic utterances produced under the influence of the Holy Spirit.

"In your heart" is the reading of KJV, TCNT, Weymouth, Knox, NEB, and others. "With your heart" is the translation of ASV and NASB. A variant of this, "with all your heart," is found in Goodspeed, RSV, and Williams. The phrase indicates that these joyful expressions are not to be merely mechanical productions of lip and finger. Unless our praise springs from the heart, it is not acceptable to the Lord.

(2) Thankfulness. The mention of joyful praise leads naturally to the mention of thanksgiving as another expression of the fullness of the Spirit. Four things are said: It is to be constant — "always." It is "for all things." It is "unto God." It is "in the name of our Lord Jesus Christ" (vs. 20). This note of thanksgiving recurs again and again in Ephesians, Colossians, and Philippians.

(3) Mutual submission. "Submitting yourselves one to another" (vs.

---

[5]Some see in the Greek word the thought of a loss of self-control. In view of the contrast drawn in this passage between drunkenness and the fullness of the Spirit, we may conclude that the Spirit-filled life is a life of moral restraint — in a word, control. See Galatians 5:23, where "self-control" is listed as part of the fruit of the Spirit.

21) denotes that attitude of reciprocal deference that becomes and marks out those who are filled with the Spirit. It is opposed to rudeness, haughtiness, selfish preference for one's own opinions, and stubborn insistence on one's own rights. Paul expressed much the same thought in Romans 12:10, "in honour preferring one another." It is an attitude that rests on the example of Him who "did not count equality with God a thing to be grasped but emptied himself, taking the form of a servant" (Phil. 2:6,7).

In verse 21 the general rule of mutual submission is stated; in 5:22–6:9 the principle is applied to specific relations. The verse thus concludes the present section and forms the connecting link with the next paragraph.

FOR FURTHER STUDY

1. Read Ephesians, marking and studying each occurrence of the word *Gentiles*.

2. Read Ephesians in a different version, marking and studying each reference to the Holy Spirit.

3. Using a concordance, study references to the Holy Spirit in Acts.

CHAPTER 10

The Daily Walk of God's New People: Domestic Obligations

(Ephesians 5:22–6:9)

If you were asked to name three or four things that today constitute the gravest threats to family life, what would your list include? Worldly concepts of marriage? Godlessness in the home? Changing views concerning sexual morality? Parental irresponsibility? The usurpation by other institutions of the prerogatives of the home? The hurried, frantic pattern of modern-day life? Television?

In a sobering chapter entitled "The Withering Away of the Family," Elton and Pauline Trueblood write, "Of all the disintegrating factors the chief is the loss of the sense of meaning of what a family ought to be. Our basic failure is not the failure to live up to a standard that is accepted, but rather the failure to keep the standard clear!" (pp. 18,19).

In this classic passage (5:22–6:9) Paul clearly delineates the standard. Beginning with the principle of mutual submission based on reverence for Christ (vs. 21), the apostle proceeds to mention the reciprocal duties of the various members of the household — wives and husbands, children and parents, slaves and masters.

I. The Wife's Duty to the Husband (5:22-24)

The only wifely duty Paul insists on is that of submission: "Wives, submit[1] yourselves unto your own husbands" (vs. 22). The RSV, NEB, NASB, and *Modern Language* have "be subject to"; Goodspeed has "subordinate yourselves to"; *The Living Bible* paraphrases it, "You wives must submit to your husbands' leadership." Clearly, Paul does not mean that the husband is to be a domestic despot, ruling his family with a rod of

---

[1]There actually is no word for "submit" in the Greek text of verse 22. The ASV and NASB show this by using italics. But whether italics are or are not used, the versions rightly insert the idea of submission, for the statement of the verse is obviously intended to be an extension and specific example of the mutual submission mentioned in the preceding verse.

iron. But he does teach that the husband exercises an authority the wife must forego. In areas where one must yield — for example, the husband's choice of a profession or of a geographical location for his work — the primary submission under ordinary conditions should devolve upon the wife.

Many people today object, saying that such a view of marriage is not appropriate for twentieth-century society. Careful consideration of the present passage, however, should remove all uneasiness about this duty of the wife to her husband.

The context clearly shows that the wife's submission is prompted by and warranted by the husband's unselfish love. No wife need have any misgivings about subordinating herself to a husband who loves her with the kind of love that Paul urges upon husbands in the verses that follow.

Moreover, the submission is to be voluntary, for the form of the Greek verb makes the statement of verse 22 something less than a positive command; it is rather an earnest appeal. The Greek word uses the middle voice, which is best translated "submitting *yourselves*." The wife's submission, then, is not something forced on her by a demanding husband; it is the deference that a loving wife, conscious that the home (just as any other institution) must have a head, gladly shows to a worthy and devoted husband.

Again, the submission of the wife is presented as a part of her Christian duty, a self-subjection to be rendered "as unto the Lord" (vs. 22; cf. Col. 3:18). The meaning is not that she is to yield to her husband the same submission she gives to Christ. The thought is that the deference given to her husband is a duty she owes to the Lord. Just as believers form one body of which Christ is head, so the married couple constitute a unity of which the husband is to be head. To ignore this divine arrangement is to sow seeds of domestic discord and tragedy.

Paul is careful to point out, however, that in one supreme respect the headship of Christ over the church differs from that of the husband over the wife. "He [the pronoun is emphatic] is the saviour of the body [i.e., the church]" (vs. 23). These words are an acknowledgment by Paul that his analogy is not perfect. Christ as Savior of His church is to the church what no husband can ever be to his wife.

The subordination of the wife to her husband is to be patterned after that of the church to Christ (vs. 24). Believers do not require the compulsion of a divine command but joyfully and willingly subject themselves to Christ. So should it be with the wife in her relation to her husband. The phrase "in every thing" is clearly limited by the context to those things pertaining to home relations. Even in this respect the rule must be qualified by the principle of allegiance to Christ. Higher obligations always take precedence over the lower.

II. THE HUSBAND'S DUTY TO THE WIFE (5:25-33)

The ancient world was a man's world, and in no place was this more apparent than in the home. Among the Jews the wife was often little more than chattel. The Greeks confined the women of the household to their own quarters and did not even permit them to eat their meals with the men. Paul's instructions are in striking contrast to all of this, for he recognizes that even the husband has duties within the home.

The supreme duty enjoined on the husband is that he love his wife (vs. 25). The word employed does not denote mere affection or romantic attachment; it speaks of a higher form of love, a deliberate attitude of mind that concerns itself with the well-being of the one loved. Self-devotion, not self-satisfaction, is its dominant trait. It is, in short, a love that should make it a delight for the wife to subject herself to such a husband. How the husband is to love his wife is set forth in three significant statements.

1. *As Christ Loved the Church* (vss. 25-27). The measure of Christ's love is stated in the declaration that He "gave himself for" the church (vs. 25). The husband is to love his wife in the same unstinted fashion, even to the point of sacrificing himself for her well-being.

The mention of Christ and the church leads Paul to digress somewhat from his discussion of marriage. He points out that there was a twofold purpose in the self-sacrifice of Jesus. The first, an immediate purpose accomplished in the present age, is "that he might sanctify and cleanse it [the church] with the washing of water by the word." "Sanctify" means to set apart, to consecrate. "Cleanse" suggests the removal of sin and its defilement. The two acts are thought of as simultaneous, the cleansing being the means by which the sanctifying is effected.

Strenuous debate has revolved around the words "with the washing of water by the word" (vs. 26). The "washing of water" is most naturally taken as a general reference to the symbolism of baptism. As an outward, physical act, it pictures the inward, spiritual cleansing effected by Christ (cf. Titus 3:5). One may understand an allusion to the symbolism of baptism without in any way subscribing to the view that baptism actually effects a spiritual cleansing. The real cleansing comes through the application of the blood of Christ by the Holy Spirit in the new birth.

The expression "by the word" is even more difficult. Some take it to refer to the word of the gospel as the actual instrument by which the cleansing is accomplished (cf. John 15:3). Others interpret it as a spoken word accompanying the washing of water — "either the word which is spoken over the person being baptized . . . (cf. Matt. 28. 19 . . .), or (more probably) the word spoken by him, in which he confesses his faith and invokes the Lord" (Bruce, p. 116; cf. Acts 22:16).

The second and ultimate purpose of Christ's death, to be realized fully at the end of the age, is set forth in verse 27: "that he might present it [the church] to himself a glorious church." The allusion is to a wedding ceremony, in which the bride is presented to her husband. The pronoun "he" stresses Christ's personal action. He himself, before the assembled universe, presents the bride to Himself. (See Rev. 19:6-9 for John's description of the scene.)

The adjective "glorious," conveying here the thought of brilliant purity or moral splendor, shows the character in which the church is to be at last manifested — "not having spot, or wrinkle, or any such thing; but that it should be holy and without blemish." When the church is presented to her Lord, there shall be nothing to mar her beauty — no spot of disfigurement, no wrinkle of age or decay, nor any other thing that might deform or defile. She is to be "holy" (i.e., consecrated) and "without blemish."

2. *As His Own Body* (vss. 28-30). Verse 28 reiterates what verses 25-27 have already said, namely, that Christ's love for His church is both model and incentive for the husband in his love for his wife. "As their own bodies" (vs. 28) gives an added reason for husbandly love. Even as Christ loves the church, His body, in like manner ought husbands to love their wives, as being their own bodies. Husband and wife are complementary parts of one personality. Hodge explains the statement thus:

> It does not indicate the measure of the husband's love, as though the meaning were, he should love his wife as much as he loves his own body. But it indicates the nature of the relation which is the ground of his love. He should love his wife, because she is his body (p. 332).

3. *With a Love Transcending All Other Human Relationships* (vss. 31-33). The love a man has for his wife must transcend even that which he has for parents, leading him to leave the latter and "be joined [glued] unto his wife" (vs. 31). So intimate is this union that the man and woman thus joined together become "one flesh" (vs. 31), which is simply a way of saying that they become "one." In a day when divorce is scandalously easy, this concept of marriage needs often to be held before the public.

The mention of the closeness of the union of husband and wife again brings to Paul's mind the thought of the intimate spiritual union of Christ and His people: "This mystery is great: but I speak in regard of Christ and of the church" (vs. 32, ASV). The word "mystery," as elsewhere in the Ephesian letter, denotes a truth once hidden but now revealed. (Cf. TEV, "There is a great truth revealed in this scripture.")

The mystery is "great" because it is both profoundly important and exceedingly wonderful.

What Paul is saying is that in the light of the gospel he sees enshrined in the statement of Genesis 2:24 a great spiritual "mystery" (truth) — Moffatt uses the expression "profound symbol" — concerning the union of Christ and His church. Verse 32b may be translated, "I for my part [the pronoun is emphatic to distinguish Paul from the writer of Genesis 2:24] am speaking with reference to Christ and with reference to the church." Thus, it is not marriage but the union between Christ and His church that Paul calls a mystery. It is the likeness of the conjugal union to this higher spiritual relationship that gives to marriage its deepest significance. Throughout the passage, Paul seems to be calling on husbands to measure up to the ideal of Christ in His love for the church, and to wives to measure up to the church in its devotion to Christ.

Verse 33 concludes Paul's discussion of marriage and calls special attention to the main point of his appeal. We may translate it in this manner: "In any case, each one of you must love his own wife as himself, and the wife must reverence [respect] her husband." The duty of the wife is to respect; the duty of the husband is to deserve that respect. The introductory phrase, "In any case" (KJV, "Nevertheless"), is used by the apostle to bring the discussion back to the matter of marriage after his lengthy digression concerning Christ and the church. It may also be Paul's way of adding that though Genesis 2:24 contains a great truth about the relation of Christ and the church, it also speaks of the relation of husband and wife. The TEV brings this out by translating, "But it [the Scripture quoted] also applies to you."

III. THE DUTY OF CHILDREN TO PARENTS (6:1-3)

Paul addresses himself to children, whose place in the home is another sphere in which the principle of submission operates. Two words sum up the child's duty to parents: "obey" and "honor." They are timely words for a day that tends to regard the freedom of the child as an absolute.

1. *Obedience* (vs. 1). The word translated "obey" implies a readiness to hear and has the sense of obeying orders. The child is to listen to, and carry out, the commands of his parents.

This obedience is a Christian duty. This thought is conveyed by the words "in the Lord" (vs. 1). They define the quality of obedience by setting forth the element or sphere in which it is to be performed. Goodspeed's rendering expresses it this way: "Children, *as Christians* obey your parents" (italics mine). A certain sacredness is thus given to the obedience rendered by the children in a Christian home. It is prompted and regulated by a consciousness of Christian responsibility and must therefore be cheerful, prompt, and habitual.

Obedience is a moral duty. Children are to obey because "this is right" (vs. 1). Filial obedience, therefore, is not based on anything accidental, nor does it depend essentially on the character of the parent.[2] It is an obligation grounded in the very nature of the relationship between parents and children. It is a thing that is right in itself.

2. *Honor* (vss. 2,3). The command to honor father and mother, quoted from the Decalogue, comprehends all the love, respect, and obedience that are involved in the filial relation. "Obedience," says Salmond, "is the duty; honour is the disposition of which the obedience is born" (p. 375). (Note that this deep respect is to be paid to both "father and mother," an indication that the wife's place in the home is not a servile one.)

This commandment to honor parents is described as "the first commandment with promise" (vs. 2). Probably Paul was thinking of the whole body of Mosaic legislation of which the Ten Commandments are the introduction. Some interpreters understand the word *first* in the sense of chief or primary: "a first commandment [i.e., one of primary importance] accompanied with a promise."

The promise itself is quoted in verse 3: "that it may be well with thee, and thou mayest live long on the earth." In their original setting (Exod. 20:12), these words apply to the nation of Israel and have specific reference to prosperity and long life in the Promised Land. Paul gives the words a wider meaning, making them apply to all children who render obedience and honor to their parents.

It would be an error, however, to apply Paul's words rigidly, for some who honor their parents die early and others who totally ignore the divine injunction may live to a ripe old age. Eadie understands Paul's use of these words to "involve a great principle, and that is, that filial obedience, under God's blessing, prolongs life, for it implies the possession of principles of restraint, sobriety, and industry, which secure a lengthened existence" (p. 442).

Hodge points out that this promise, like all other such promises, "is a revelation of a general purpose of God, and makes known what will be the usual course of his providence. . . . Obedient children, as a general rule, are prosperous and happy. The general promise is fulfilled to individuals, just so far as it shall serve for God's glory, and their own good" (p. 359).

---

[2]It should be observed, however, that the entire passage concerns relationships within the Christian family; Paul therefore does not contemplate unchristian attitudes on the part of parents.

IV. THE DUTY OF PARENTS TO CHILDREN (6:4)

Parental responsibility is stated in terms of the father's obligation. The suggestion is that the father as head of the household has a special responsibility in regard to the training of the children. No slight toward the mother is intended. Paul would be quick to recognize her rights and to acknowledge the molding power of her influence in the home. It is even possible that the word "fathers" is used in the broad sense of "parents," as it obviously is in the Greek text of Hebrews 11:23.

It is said that Martin Luther's father was so stern that Luther found it difficult to pray, "Our Father." To him the word *father* had a connotation of forbidding severity. "Spare the rod and spoil the child" he took to be wise counsel, but to keep others from having his own unpleasant childhood experience, he suggested keeping an apple beside the rod to give the child when he does well.

The authority of parents is for the child's good, not for the parents' own selfish gratification. To make unreasonable demands of a child, to surround him with needless restrictions, or to punish him too severely will deaden his affections toward the parents and check his desire after holiness. Many a child has reached the point where he feels he cannot possibly please his parents and therefore decides that he need not try. It is a wise parent who seeks to make obedience easy for his children.

On the positive side, fathers are charged to bring up their children "in the nurture and admonition of the Lord" (vs. 4). The word translated "bring up" conveys here the idea of development in character. Weymouth sees in the word a connotation of tenderness. The word for "nurture" was used by the ancient Greeks of the general education of a child, of the whole course of training by which a boy was reared into a man. Moule understands it in the present text to include all "the wholesome *restraints* of a wise early education," "all training in the direction of a life modest, unselfish, and controlled" (*Cambridge Bible*, p. 146).

"Admonition" is a term containing the ideas of correction and warning, both of which parents owe to their children. The words "of the Lord" show that the training and correction of the child are to be exercised in a thoroughly Christian manner. It is training and correction administered by the parents, but proceeding from the Lord. The suggestion is that the Lord nurtures the child through the parents.

V. THE DUTY OF SLAVES TO MASTERS (6:5-8)

The "servants" mentioned in this passage were bond servants, or slaves, not servants in the modern sense of the word. Slavery, with all its attendant evils, was universally accepted in ancient times. In fact, it was considered a fundamental institution, indispensable to civilized society.

More than half the people seen on the streets of some of the great cities of the Roman world were slaves. It has been estimated that there were as many as 60,000,000 of them in the Roman Empire. Included among them were laborers, domestic servants, clerks, teachers, doctors, and other professional people. They were people without rights, mere property existing only for the comfort, convenience, and pleasure of their owners. (Many of them were better educated and more cultured than their masters and were charged with the instruction of the children of the household.) Doubtless, the early Christian churches numbered many slaves among their members.

It is a surprise to some people that the apostles did not denounce slavery in unequivocal language and demand its immediate overthrow. But the apostles did not conceive of themselves primarily as social reformers; they were first and foremost heralds of the good news of salvation in Christ. Yet they did not condone slavery. Indeed, they announced the very principles (such as that of the complete spiritual equality of slave and master) that ultimately destroyed this terrible blot on civilization. The apostles' approach to this social evil was like that of a woodsman who strips the bark off a tree and leaves it to die. John Eadie wrote:

> Christianity did not rudely assault the forms of social life, or seek to force even a justifiable revolution by external appliances. Such an enterprise would have quenched the infant religion in blood. The gospel achieved a nobler feat. It did not stand by in disdain, and refuse to speak to the slave till he gained his freedom, and the shackles fell from his arms. . . . No; but it went down into his degradation, took him by the hand, uttered words of kindness in his ear, and gave him a liberty which fetters could not abridge and tyranny could not suppress (p. 446).

A study of the present passage, as well as similar passages in Colossians (3:22–4:1), 1 Peter (3:18-25), and Philemon (especially vs. 16), reveals that the New Testament writers sought to give the slaves a sense of dignity in their work and to comfort them in their suffering. Moreover, they sought to regulate the institution among their own people by reminding Christian masters that they should treat their slaves with fairness and kindness.

In the passage now under consideration Paul at the very outset points out that the slave/master relationship belongs only to the sphere of earthly things. The phrase "masters according to the flesh" (vs. 5) implies another relationship belonging to a higher, spiritual sphere where Christ is Master.

1. *The Manner in Which Obedience Is to Be Performed* (vss. 5-7). The one duty urged on slaves was that of obedience. They were to obey "with fear and trembling" (vs. 5). These words were probably not

intended to express an attitude of abject terror, but rather the solicitous spirit of one having a true sense of responsibility and therefore eager to leave no duty undone. The TCNT uses the expression "anxious care." Goodspeed has "reverence and awe."

Obedience was to be given "in singleness of . . . heart" (vs. 5). That is, it was to be done with inward reality and sincerity, without duplicity and pretense. TCNT understands the Greek to denote "ungrudging service."

Obedience was to be "as unto Christ" (vs. 5). This means that the slave was to look upon his obedience to his earthly master as a kind of Christian duty, a service performed as to the Lord Himself. This point of view would lift the most menial task to the highest level and constitute strong motivation for carrying it out.

Verses 6,7 explain still further what it would mean for slaves to serve in the manner just described. Verse 6a states the matter negatively: They would not perform their duties "with eyeservice, as menpleasers." "Eyeservice" graphically depicts the conduct of the person who works only when he is watched. Such persons are "menpleasers," that is, workmen whose highest aim is to curry favor with their masters. Verses 6b, 7 state the matter positively: Those who serve aright perform their duties "as the servants [slaves] of Christ, doing the will of God from the heart; with good will doing service, as to the Lord, and not to men." The believing slave was to see himself as Christ's slave and to understand that in the performance of his daily tasks he was doing God's will. For this reason his work was to be done heartily (literally, "out of the soul") and with "good will," that is, cheerfully.

If Paul could write in this manner of the work of a person enslaved against his will, he would in even stronger language address himself to the modern-day employee who voluntarily enters into contract with an employer and receives remuneration for his work. Surely, all that is said here of the fidelity and sincerity of slave service must with even greater force apply to free service.

2. *An Incentive for Obedience* (vs. 8). The participle "knowing" (vs. 8) has causal force, and gives encouragement to the faithful performance of slave service. Earthly masters might take no note of faithful service rendered to them. But the Christian slave can know that his heavenly Master will not fail to recompense his work. Every "good thing" done, whether by "bond or free," is known to the Lord and shall of His grace be rewarded.

VI. THE DUTY OF MASTERS TO SLAVES (6:9)

Duty was not all on the side of slaves; Paul reminded masters that they also had obligations. In so doing, he was giving expression to a very radical idea, for in that day it was commonly thought that slaves had no rights. Verse 9 contains three things: a principle, a prohibition, and an incentive for heeding these words of the apostle.

The *principle* is stated generally: "Ye masters, do the same things unto them." That is to say, act toward your slaves with the same regard to the will of God and the authority of Christ as has been enjoined on them.

The *prohibition* is against "threatening." Such an admonition was most appropriate, for the common idea was that slaves must be kept in check by the fear of punishment. Christian masters must leave off this evil practice entirely. Those under their authority are to be treated always with respect and kindness, never with harshness. Does this admonition not say something regarding the treatment twentieth-century employers should give to those who work for them? Surely nothing less that the consideration enjoined on slaveholders becomes a present-day employer.

The *incentive* for acting in this manner might be rendered: "since you know that both their Master and yours is in heaven . . ." (vs. 9b). Christian masters are accountable to God for their treatment of slaves. Both they and their slaves bow alike before one Master, with whom there is no "respect of persons." The latter phrase denotes partiality or favoritism. The TCNT takes it in this context to speak of "distinction of rank." Eadie's comment is apropos: "The gold ring of the master does not attract His eye, and it is not averted from the iron fetter of the slave."

For Further Study

1. Compare Ephesians 5:22–6:9 with Colossians 3:18–4:1.

2. Thoughtfully and prayerfully consider your own home life in light of the things said in Ephesians 5:22–6:4.

3. Take a hymnal and look for songs relating to the home. Read especially J. P. Spitta's "O Happy Home Where Thou Art Loved" and Henry Ware's "Happy the Home When God Is There."

4. Using a concordance, study the New Testament occurrences of the expression "respect of persons" (or "partiality").

CHAPTER 11

The Holy Warfare of God's New People

(Ephesians 6:10-24)

It is a grave mistake to think that in the happy hour of our conversion all trouble and strife cease. In reality, that hour marks the beginning of a lifelong warfare — not a war for our salvation, to be sure, but a war in Christian service. The closing portion of Paul's letter contains his account of this conflict of the Christian with the forces of evil.

I. The Christian Warfare (6:10-20)

A note of tranquility pervades most of Ephesians. Beginning with a doxology of praise to God for the blessings of redemption, it proceeds to speak of the electing grace of God, the wonder of spiritual resurrection in Christ, the blissful indwelling of Christ in His people, and the pure and holy lives they are to live. The Epistle closes, however, amid the din of battle with a rousing call to arms. For all the joys and for all the peace and happiness of the Christian life, it is nonetheless a life lived out on a spiritual battlefield.

Some commentators liken the Christian experience to life within a camp located in enemy territory. Within the camp the scene is one of loyalty, love, and fellowship. The ramparts, however, cannot for a moment be left unwatched. The saint must never live and move unarmed.

In the preceding section Christians have been singled out by groups, with special counsel for each. But what is said here is for all. Like a general leading an army against the enemy, Paul issues commands and gives instructions. He mentions the believer's strength (vs. 10), his foe (vs. 12), and his protection (vss. 11,13-17).

1. *The Believer's Strength* (vs. 10). As Paul thinks of the inevitable conflict, he charges Christians to be constantly filled with power. The word used, a particularly strong one suggesting the pouring of power into one, occurs also in Philippians 4:13: "I can do all things through

125

Christ which strengtheneth [pours power into] me." The source of the strength needed is brought out by "in the Lord," the idea being that by virtue of our union with Him the power that is inherently His may be drawn upon by us. In Him we can do all things; apart from Him, defeat is inevitable.

What it means to be strong in the Lord is further explained by the phrase "and in the power of his might." To be strong in the Lord is to be joined to the strength that belongs to His might. Observe the two leading words: "power" and "might." The former, which is used in the New Testament only of supernatural power — whether Satanic (Heb. 2:14) or divine (everywhere else) — denotes power as an active force, as power exercised. The latter word, more passive in meaning, speaks of strength inherently possessed, whether exercised or not. This impressive accumulation of terms for strength, power, and might recalls 1:19, where Paul describes the exceeding greatness of the power of God available to believing people. Here, the readers are urgently exhorted to lay hold on that power in order to meet and vanquish the evil forces that assail them.

2. *The Believer's Foe* (vs. 12). In military strategy the failure to estimate properly the strength and capabilities of an enemy is a tragic mistake. In the Christian confrontation it is not only tragic but inexcusable, for we are clearly warned both of the nature of the conflict and of the formidable character of the enemy. "We wrestle not against flesh and blood." We are engaged in a life-and-death struggle, not against a frail human enemy but against the supernatural forces of evil. The word translated "we wrestle" suggests hand-to-hand combat and thus magnifies the personal nature of the encounter.

"Principalities," "powers," "rulers," and "spiritual wickedness" are terms used here of the hierarchy of the invisible powers in rebellion against God (cf. 1:21; 3:10). Paul is not to be understood as enumerating four different classes of demonic beings. Each term simply views the forces arrayed against God and His people in a different manner. "Principalities" refers to their rank and rule. "Powers" suggests their investment with authority. "World-rulers of this darkness" (ASV) points up their control over a world in revolt against its Creator (cf. 2 Cor. 4:4). "Spiritual wickedness in high places" (ASV, "spiritual hosts of wickedness in the heavenly places") depicts them as an army of wicked spirits inhabiting, or at least bringing their combat to, the heavenly sphere.

The phrase "in the heavenlies" (cf. 1:3,20; 2:6; 3:10) may be interpreted as the scene of the conflict. So understood, the reference is to the heavenly sphere in which life in Christ is lived. The phrase may mean that the abode of the spiritual forces of wickedness is nonearthly, belonging to the invisible regions of the spirit world.

3. *The Believer's Protection* (vss. 11, 13-20). In another place Paul asserts that "the weapons of our warfare are not of the flesh, but mighty before God to the casting down of strongholds" (2 Cor. 10:4, ASV). Here he asserts that the Christian finds protection in this mortal conflict by the use of the whole armor of God (vss. 11,13-17) and the practice of incessant prayer (vss. 18-20).

(1) The whole armor of God (vss. 11,13-17). The expression "whole armour of God" (vss. 11,13) employs the imagery of the Roman man of arms fully equipped for heavy battle. It is the armor "of God" in the sense that it is armor that God provides. Each piece is furnished by Him. It is called "the whole" armor to stress the completeness of it. We must see to it that no portion of our person is left exposed and unprotected.

God provides the armor, and it is ready for our use. But it is we who must, on our part, faithfully accept every instrument and implement that God offers. We are therefore urged to "put on" the whole armor of God in order that we "may be able to stand against the wiles of the devil" (vs. 11). The tense of the verb "put on" denotes urgent and decisive action. When we have already engaged the enemy, it will be too late to arm ourselves. "To stand" means, in this context, not only to stand ready to fight, but to hold one's ground. The "wiles of the devil" are his stratagems, the many and subtle ways by which he assails God's people. The TEV uses the expression "the Devil's evil tricks." (See the use of "wiles" in 4:14, ASV.)

In verse 13 "wherefore" points back to the descriptions of verse 12 and calls attention to the menacing character of the enemy. He is so formidable in power that nothing less than the full armor of God will give ample protection. Instead of "put on," Paul here writes "take up" (ASV), the more common military expression for arming oneself. The suggestion is that the divine armor lies at the believer's feet ready for use; it needs only to be appropriated by him. The tense is again such as to denote urgency. Arms must be taken up at once in order for the Christian to be ready for any emergency.

The particular end in view is that the Christian "may be able to withstand in the evil day, and having done all, to stand" (vs. 13). The word rendered "to withstand" means to resist successfully. The "evil day" refers to those critical days of special trial or resolute satanic assault known to every child of God. As Maclaren observes, they are the days "when all the cannon belch at once, and scaling ladders are reared on every side of the fortress." The great preacher goes on to say that these days "are ever wont to come on us suddenly; they are heralded by no storm signals and no falling barometer. We may be like soldiers sitting securely round their camp fire, till all at once bullets begin to fall among them." Against such days we must always be ready.

"Having done all" is a particularly strong expression meaning "having thoroughly done everything." (Cf. TCNT, "having fought to the end.") The reference is not to the preparation for conflict but to the end of the conflict, when the enemy has been thoroughly vanquished. "To stand" speaks of the stance of victory. The thought is that the well-armed believer will be able to hold his ground. After the conflict is over, he does not lie prostrate in defeat but *stands* — in complete possession of the field.

Salmond explains the idea in this fashion: "The spiritual warrior who has kept his position victorious and stood above his conquered foe in one 'evil day,' is to take his stand again ready to face another such critical day, should it come."[1] What is necessary to such a stand is expressed by four participles (ASV), each of which modifies the imperative "stand." These participles — "having girded" (vs. 14), "having put on" (vs. 14), "having shod" (vs. 15), and "taking up" (vs. 16) — speak of things that are to be done before one takes his stand.

The first piece of defensive armor is the girdle of truth (vs. 14). The soldier's girdle was the belt or band that served to hold his tunic in place and from which the scabbard for his sword was suspended. "Truth" is without the article in the Greek text and therefore carries the idea of sincerity and truthfulness. It should be remembered, however, that this disposition of sincerity and truthfulness is not a natural quality; it is a supernatural grace, for the whole armor is of God.

Another essential part of the Roman soldier's equipment was the "breastplate," which, as its name suggests, protected the vital organs in the chest area. Without a breastplate a warrior was vulnerable to every assault of the enemy. Paul says that "righteousness" is the Christian's breastplate (vs. 14). This righteousness is sometimes understood to be the righteousness of justification, that which Paul elsewhere calls "the righteousness which is of God by faith" (Phil. 3:9). The word may here be used, however, in a broad, general sense of moral rectitude, meaning the believer's personal righteousness. This personal righteousness that guards the heart is not possible apart from the reception of God's justifying righteousness.

The well-equipped soldier in Paul's day wore sandals with soles thickly studded with hobnails. Such sandals not only gave protection to the feet but also enabled the soldier to move quickly and surely. In ancient times, when warfare was largely a matter of hand-to-hand com-

---

[1]S. D. F. Salmond, *The Epistle to the Ephesians.* The Expositor's Greek Testament (Grand Rapids: Wm. B. Eerdmans Publishing Company, n.d.).

bat, this quickness of movement was essential. The Christian, Paul explains, must have on his feet "the preparation of the gospel of peace" (vs. 15). Most interpreters understand "preparation" in the sense of "readiness" to serve God. The idea is that of a disposition of mind that makes men quick to see their duty and ever ready to plung into the fight. This readiness comes from, or is produced by, "the gospel of peace."

The gospel is so designated because it is a peace-bringing power that destroys the enemity in men's hearts and establishes tranquility in its place (cf. Isa. 52:7). It is this heart-peace produced by the gospel that gives the Christian warrior his readiness for combat. To have a consciousness of peace with God and to live in tranquil communion with Him enables one to fling himself into the battle with strong determination and calm assurance.

Next, Paul names "the shield of [or, which is] faith," which "above all" is to be taken up. "Above all" means simply "in addition to all." (A variant reading of the Greek text, preferred by many scholars, employs a preposition that requires the phrase to be translated "in all things." If this reading is followed, the meaning then must be that the shield is to be taken up at every turn of the conflict. Compare TCNT, "At every onslaught take up faith for your shield.")

The "shield of faith" is an allusion not to the small round shield that was carried by cavalrymen but to the large oblong shield that the heavily-armed soldier carried. Behind it a man was fully protected. And that is the kind of shield, says Paul, that our conflict requires.

The "fiery darts" — among the most dangerous weapons used in ancient warfare — were arrows dipped in pitch or some other combustible material and set on fire before being thrown at the enemy. They could not only wound but also burn. The soldier's best protection — indeed, his only real protection — was to manipulate his shield so that these flaming missiles sank into its wood. Thus the missile was stopped and its fire was extinguished. "Faith," by which we must understand utter dependence on God, affords like protection for the believer when he confronts Satan's most vicious attacks.

Faith protects us, however, not so much because of any inherent power it has but because it brings us into touch with God and interposes Him between the enemy and ourselves. By faith, therefore, we are enabled "to quench all the fiery darts of the wicked [one]," that is, the devil. Pay special attention to the word *all*. In it there is ground for great confidence — not in ourselves, to be sure, but in God and in the strength that reliance on Him gives.

The last piece of defensive equipment to be named is "the helmet of [or, which is] salvation" (vs. 17). Since Paul is addressing Christians, the reference must be to the *consciousness* of salvation and the protection that such consciousness gives. The Christian warrior is commanded to "take" the helmet of salvation. This word, which is not the same as that used in reference to the shield, ordinarily means "to receive," "accept," or "welcome." In the present passage, however, it probably means "grasp."

The "sword of [supplied by] the Spirit" (vs. 17) is the only offensive weapon in the panoply. But no other is needed. By it, Christian (in Bunyan's allegory) put Apollyon to flight, and we will find it more than adequate to meet our needs. In the last clause of verse 17 it is identified with "the word of God." This expression, the Greek of which more literally means "God's utterance," is not necessarily to be confined to the Bible. When Paul wrote this passage, much of the New Testament had not yet come into being, and the Spirit was still speaking directly to the redeemed community apart from the written revelation (cf. Acts 11:28; 21:10,11; 1 Cor. 14). However, the use our Lord made of the written Word in His wilderness temptation lends strong support to the view that the primary and abiding application of Paul's phrase must be to the believing use of the Scriptures as a mighty weapon in the conflict with evil. Christian experience tends to confirm this view.

(2) The practice of prayer (vss. 18-20). Two words are here used for the believer's prayerful approach to God. "Prayer," the more-inclusive term, is general enough to include the whole act of worship. "Supplication," narrower in its scope, is petitionary prayer. A sharp distinction in meaning, however, is not always to be insisted on. The use of both words here appears mainly to add intensity to the thought. The words "with all [i.e., every kind of] prayer and supplication," which in the Greek precede "praying always," are to be construed with "stand" (vs. 14). Prayer is the means by which the Christian takes his stand and is the spirit or temper in which he confronts the enemy and puts him to flight.

There are times in a Christian's warfare when he feels unable to use even the sword of the Spirit as an effective weapon. Recall Bunyan's account of the experience of Christian in the Valley of the Shadow of Death. About in the middle of that valley he found a place he perceived to be "the mouth of hell." "And ever and anon," wrote Bunyan, "the flame and smoke would come out in such abundance, with sparks and hideous noises (things that cared not for Christian's sword, as did Apollyon before), that he was forced to put up his sword, and betake himself to another weapon, called 'All-Prayer.' " When thus he wielded this mighty weapon, the fiends of hell "gave back and came no farther." So must we also at every phase of the conflict enlist the aid of our all-powerful God. In response to our urgent prayer, He comes as a mighty ally to stand by our side.

Paul speaks of the *manner* of prayer and its *objects*. With reference to the former, the apostle teaches that it is to be offered "always" (literally, "in every season," vs. 18). The reference is not so much to prayer that is "without ceasing" (1 Thess. 5:17) as it is to crisis prayer — prayer on every occasion of conflict, prayer in "the evil day." In such times of dire need we must cry to God with special intensity. Again, we are to pray "in the Spirit" — under His influence and with His gracious assistance (cf. Rom. 8:26; Jude 20). And finally, such earnest supplication requires vigilance and perseverance: "watching . . . with all perseverance and supplication" (vs. 18). "Watching" translates a word that literally means "to keep awake" and in this context conveys the thought of never being off guard. "Perseverance" suggests persistency, the opposite of growing weary and giving up.

For what, or for whom, are we to pray? First, and generally, we pray "for all saints" (vs. 18). "No soldier entering battle," says Hodge (in loc.), "prays for himself alone, but for all his fellow-soldiers also. They form one army, and the success of one is the success of all." The appeal is especially appropriate for our day, when so many believing people, living under governments antagonistic to the gospel, are being viciously assaulted by the enemy. Let us expand our vision and enlarge our hearts so as to encompass in our prayers these and other sorely tried Christians.

Second, and more specifically, Paul requested prayer for himself (vss. 19,20). At two points he particularly needed this. One was "that utterance" might "be given" to him when he opened his mouth to speak (vs. 19). Paul's hope was that even as a prisoner he might boldly "make known the mystery (TCNT, 'inmost truth'] of the gospel" (vs. 19). The second request is similar: Remembering that for the sake of the gospel he was "an ambassador" — and this in spite of his "bonds" (chains) — he was anxious that in making known the gospel he should speak with the boldness and confidence that became his high commission from the court of heaven (vs. 20).

II. The Conclusion of the Letter (6:21-24)

The apostle brings his majestic Epistle to a close. Nothing remains to be said save a few parting words of explanation and the benediction.

1. *An Explanation* (vss. 21,22). The concluding explanation concerns Tychicus and his special mission for Paul. This man the apostle highly commends as "a beloved brother and faithful minister in the Lord." (See also Acts 20:4; Col. 4:7; 2 Tim. 4:12; and Titus 3:12. From

these references we learn, among other things, that Tychicus was an Asian, a man of high character, and a trusted companion of Paul.) His is the only personal name appearing in Ephesians, apart, of course, from those of Paul and our Lord. We may gather from the present passage that he was the bearer of this letter to its destination. In addition to this responsibility, he was to give firsthand information to the recipients of the Epistle concerning Paul's circumstances. In so doing, he was to comfort or encourage their hearts (vss. 21,22).

2. *A Benediction* (vss. 23,24). The benediction, which actually is in two parts, gathers up several of the great words of this Epistle — peace, love, faith, and grace — and expresses the apostle's fervent desire that the readers may experience with increasing fullness the reality symbolized by these words.

The final phrase of the letter, in which Paul speaks of the recipients of grace as "them that love our Lord Jesus Christ in sincerity" (vs. 24), is full of interest. Mark the breadth of it — "all them that love our Lord." In the apostle's view all who do in truth love the Lord — whatever their race, nationality, or standing in society — are in vital contact with the grace of God, and all believing people may call them brothers. The words thus echo the emphasis on spiritual oneness that has pervaded so much of the letter.

Note the solemn fullness with which Paul speaks of the Savior. Calling him "our Lord Jesus Christ," the apostle draws attention to the sovereignty, the humanity, and the redemptive office of our incarnate Savior. A Christian is one who knows Jesus and loves Him in all these aspects of His being.

Finally, one must not miss the force of the last word of the Epistle, translated in KJV by "sincerity," but more accurately rendered "incorruptibility." It is a term rich in meaning (cf. 1 Cor. 9:25; 15:52; 1 Tim. 1:17). Here it characterizes the love of believers for their Lord as having an enduring, deathless quality. It is a fitting word with which to close this sublime Epistle.

FOR FURTHER STUDY

1. Read John Bunyan's *Pilgrim's Progress*. If you do not own a copy, consider buying one. Charles Spurgeon thought so highly of this Christian classic that he read it more than one hundred times.

2. Make your own list of the various parts of the Christian's armor.

3. Evaluate this statement: "Reduced to its essence . . . the 'panoply' [whole armor] means — Jesus Christ. The soldier, in other words, appears before us made strong for a victory which is otherwise

impossible — by his relation to his Lord" (Moule, *Ephesian Studies*, p. 326).

4. Read through Ephesians and make a list of all the teachings concerning the person and work of Jesus Christ. For example: He is the Son of God (1:3; 4:13); He is the Beloved One (1:6); we are accepted in Him (1:6); and in Him we have redemption and forgiveness (1:7).

Bibliography

Barclay, William. *The Letters to the Galatians and Ephesians*. Philadelphia: The Westminster Press, 1958.

Blaikie, W. G. *Ephesians*. The Pulpit Commentary. New York: Funk and Wagnalls, n.d.

Beare, F. W. *The Epistle to the Ephesians*. The Interpreter's Bible. New York: Abingdon-Cokesbury Press, n.d.

Brown, Charles. *St. Paul's Epistles to the Ephesians*. A Devotional Commentary. London: The Religious Tract Society, 1911.

Bruce, F. F. *The Epistle to the Ephesians*. New York: Fleming H. Revell Company, 1961.

Calvin, John. *Commentaries on the Epistles of Paul to the Galatians and the Ephesians*, trans. William Pringle. Grand Rapids: Wm. B. Eerdmans Publishing Company, 1918.

Carver, W. O. *The Glory of God in the Christian Calling*. Nashville: Broadman Press, 1949.

Denney, James. *The Death of Christ*. London: Hodder and Stoughton, 1907.

Eadie, John. *Commentary on the Epistle to the Ephesians*, reprint ed. Grand Rapids: Zondervan Publishing House, n.d.

Erdman, Charles R. *Commentaries on the New Testament: Ephesians*. Philadelphia: Westminster Press, 1931.

Farrar, F. W. *The Message of the Books*. New York: E. P. Dutton and Company, 1885.

Findlay, George G. *The Epistle to the Ephesians*. The Expositor's Bible. New York: George H. Doran Company, n.d.

Hendricksen, William. *Exposition of Ephesians*. New Testament Commentary. Grand Rapids: Baker Book House, 1967.

Hodge, Charles. *A Commentary on the Epistle to the Ephesians*, reprint ed. Grand Rapids: Wm. B. Eerdmans Publishing Company, 1950.

Hunter, A. M. *The Layman's Bible Commentary*. Richmond: John Knox Press, 1959.

Jowett, John Henry. *The Passion for Souls*. New York: Fleming H. Revell Company, 1905.

Lenski, R. C. H. *The Interpretation of St. Paul's Epistles to the Galatians, to the Ephesians, and to the Philippians*. Columbus, Ohio: The Wartburg Press, 1946.

Mackay, John. *God's Order: The Ephesian Letter and This Present Time*. New York: The Macmillan Company, 1953.

Maclaren, Alexander. *Expositions of Holy Scripture*, vol. 10, reprint ed. Grand Rapids: Wm. B. Eerdmans Publishing Company, 1942.

Moule, H. C. G. *Ephesian Studies*. New York: Fleming H. Revell Company, n.d.

————. *The Epistle to the Ephesians*. The Cambridge Bible for Schools and Colleges. Cambridge: The University Press, 1887.

Moulton, Harold K. *Colossians, Philemon and Ephesians*. Epworth Preacher's Commentaries. London: The Epworth Press, 1963.

Robinson J. Armitage. *St. Paul's Epistle to the Ephesians*. London: James Clarke & Co. Ltd., n.d.

Rowley, H. H. *The Biblical Doctrine of Election*. London: Lutterworth Press, 1950.

Salmond. S. D. F. *The Epistle to the Ephesians*. The Expositor's Greek Testament. Grand Rapids: Wm. B. Eerdmans Publishing Company, n.d.

Scroggie, Graham. *Paul's Prison Prayers*. London: Pickering and Inglis; Ltd., n.d.

Simpson. E. K. *Commentary on the Epistle to the Ephesians*. The New International Commentary on the New Testament. Grand Rapids: Wm. B. Eerdmans Publishing Company, 1957.

Smith, Justin A. *Commentary on the Epistle to the Ephesians*. An American Commentary on the New Testament. Philadelphia: The American Baptist Publication Society, n.d.

Spurgeon, Charles H. *The Treasury of the Bible: New Testament*, vol. 3. Grand Rapids: Zondervan Publishing House, n.d.

Summers, Ray. *Ephesians: Pattern for Christian Living*. Nashville: Broadman Press, 1960.

Trueblood, Elton and Pauline. *The Recovery of Family Life*. New York: Harper and Row, Publishers, Inc., 1953.

Vine, W. E. *Expository Dictionary of New Testament Words*. New York: Fleming H. Revell Company, 1966.

Wescott, B. F. *St. Paul's Epistle to the Ephesians*. Grand Rapids: Wm. B. Eerdmans Publishing Company, 1950.

All biblical quotations are from the King James Version unless otherwise indicated. Other translations referred to are as follows:

Good News for Modern Man: The New Testament in Today's English Version. New York: American Bible Society, n.d. Referred to in the Study Guide as TEV.

Goodspeed, Edgar J. *The New Testament: An American Translation.* Chicago: The University of Chicago Press, 1951.

Knox, Ronald. *The Holy Bible: A Translation from the Latin Vulgate in the Light of the Hebrew and Greek Originals.* New York: Sheed and Ward, Inc. , 1956.

Moffatt, James. *The New Testament: A New Translation.* New York: Harper and Brothers, 1950.

New American Standard Bible. Nashville: Broadman Press, 1960. Referred to in the Study Guide as NASB.

New International Version: New Testament. Grand Rapids: Zondervan Bible Publishers, 1973. Referred to in the Study Guide as NIV.

Phillips, J. B. *The New Testament in Modern English.* New York: The Macmillan Company, 1962.

The Living Bible: Paraphrased. Wheaton, Illinois: Tyndale House Publishers, 1971.

The Modern Language Bible. The New Berkeley Version. Grand Rapids: Zondervan Publishing House, 1959.

The New American Bible. New York: P. J. Kenedy and Sons, 1970. Referred in the Study Guide as NAB.

The New English Bible. Oxford and Cambridge: University Press, 1965. Referred to in the Study Guide as NEB.

The Holy Bible: Revised Standard Version. New York: National Council of Churches of Christ, 1952. Referred to in the Study Guide as RSV.

The Holy Bible: American Standard Edition. New York: Thomas Nelson and Sons, 1929. Referred to in the Study Guide as ASV.

The Twentieth Century New Testament: A Translation into Modern English. Chicago: Moody Press, n.d. Referred to in the Study Guide as TCNT.

Weymouth, Richard Francis. *The New Testament in Modern Speech.* Newly revised by James Alexander Robertson. New York: Harper and Brothers, n.d.

Williams, Charles B. *The New Testament: A Private Translation in the Language of the People.* Chicago: Moody Press, 1949.